THE WAY
IT WAS...

BY: MALACHY DONOGHUE

INTRODUCTION

I am truly grateful to my patient and loving wife, Maureen – without her cooperation, this story would never have been written.

On many occasions, Maureen would say, "It's a shame you don't write about your experiences of growing up in Ireland during and after World War II, and your eventual arrival in the U.S.A and your life thereafter."

Sometime later our son Mike approached me and said, "You know Dad; you have had so many diverse experiences in your life that I think would be worth writing about. Please consider doing this – I feel it would make a very interesting story."

After giving this some thought, I agreed figuring this would be a simple task. Little did I know how complicated my life had been and when I began, I had absolutely no idea where this was going.

Once I started, names, dates, people and places kept pouring out as if it all happened yesterday. So much of this was long, long forgotten – buried in my subconscious all those years.

Writing about my life was much more challenging than I expected but…that's the way it was..

CHAPTER 1

Mornings like this would make you feel like you were in heaven. It was June 27, 1939 and it was a typical, beautiful summer's morning in Ireland. The sun was burning through the early morning mist, the dew was sparkling on the grass and the air had a slight chill that made you know you were alive.

My sister, Chris, and I were preparing to leave for school. All that was left to do was put our book bags on our two bicycles and we would be on our way. As I was passing my parents' bedroom, my dad called me and asked if it was nine o'clock yet. Those were the last words he would ever speak to me – by eleven o'clock he was dead.

My life would never be the same again. Little did I know that day would shape my future forever. This was the end of my childhood – Malachy Donoghue was propelled into an eleven year old adult.

The village that I was born in, named Knockcroghery in the county of Roscommon, Ireland received its name from "Cnoc-an-Crochaire", which is the Gaelic translation of "Hill of the Hangman". This hill, which is located east of the village, was once used as a place of execution, where many lives were taken. Folklore indicates that justice, or injustice, as the case may have been, was swift and severe.

Knockcroghery was known for its clay pipe factory that was in production for over two hundred and fifty years. These clay pipes were used for the smoking of tobacco and were particularly popular at "Irish Wakes" where they were filled with tobacco and given to the mourners. Production ceased abruptly on June 19, 1921. The village was set ablaze by the Black and Tans (a division of the British Army) during the War of Independence. This branch was known for their cruelty - they robbed, plundered, and murdered and what they couldn't take – they burned. That is what happened to this little village – they burned it to the ground and when they withdrew, there was nothing left but a smoldering pile of rubble.

There must have been a root cause for the British Army to act with such a vengeance and even though I grew up living among many of the survivors, I never learned what possibly could have triggered such a horrendous act.

My mother often talked about her experience with the Black and Tans when she was a young girl. Her brother, Johnny, was a Captain in the Irish Republican Army and was wanted by the British. In the dead of night, they would surround her home, pound on the door and rouse everyone from their beds. They would drag her, her parents, brothers and sisters in their night clothes from their warm beds to the outside. Then they would line them up against the wall and put the cold, steel muzzles of their rifles up to their temples and threaten to blow their brains out if they didn't tell them where John Gately was. They would ransack the house in search of him and those surprise searches would be repeated over and over again – day and night. Fortunately they were never able to locate him.

My dad lived in the U.S. prior to WWI and was a successful businessman. He owned several saloons and invested in real estate. He fought with the American forces during the war and after the war ended, he took a trip back to Ireland and met my mom.

After they were married, they returned to the United States in 1922 and lived on Central Park West in the 80s in an apartment building that my dad owned.

My mom had difficulty adjusting to city life – she was very homesick and missed the peace and quiet of living in the country. My brother, Jimmy and my sister, Maureen were born in New York City and in 1925 my parents returned to Ireland.

They purchased property in Knockcroghery and on it built a house with a bar and grocery store connected to it. That is where the remaining children were born.

There were nine children in our family and I was the fourth born. Their names in birth rotation are: Jimmy, Maureen, Christine, Malachy, Kevin, Eamon, Catherine, John and Anita. My parents were American Citizens so the seven of us that were born in Ireland were all born American Citizens – the term used was "Derivative Citizenship – or born abroad of American parents".

By the time I was born the village had been completely re-built and had grown to five stores of various types, a Catholic Church, a Protestant Church, a Dance Hall, a Post Office and a two-room school house to be used as a grammar school and a Rail Road Station. My father always regretted having left the states – he loved the excitement of the business world in New York and one of the bars that he owned remained in the family until 1947, which was later owned by my mother's brother, Mike Gately. This is my uncle that I worked for when I came to the United States.

The village, unfortunately, was very political and the schoolmaster and my dad belonged to two opposing political parties and as a result of their differences in politics my dad took my sister Christine and myself out of the local school and sent us to another grammar school which was at least three miles away from where we lived. This meant we had to ride our bicycles to and from school everyday so it may have been a small village but politics played a very big part in it.

Maureen was in high school at this point so she wasn't involved. Our older brother, Jimmy, died in 1932 at the age of 9 years and 9 months from Spinal Meningitis. That was also the year my Uncle Malachy, my mother's brother, was ordained an African Missionary Priest so that was a bittersweet year for our family.

My best friend, also named Malachy, lived across the street from us. His name was Malachy Murray. He was known as Malack and I was called Malachy – that's how they told us apart. We were inseparable and had a lot of fun together – we loved to play handball, football, and soccer.

We would go around to the four bars in the village and behind the bars all the empty bottles would be stored. There were whiskey bottles, brandy bottles, sherry bottles and beer bottles and we would drain them and mix all the liquid together and put it in one bottle. Then we would go over to Malack's yard where the hens and the chickens were and one of us would hold the hen or the chicken's mouth open and the other would pour the booze down their necks. We would keep this up until we ran out of liquor and then we would let the chickens loose out in the yard and we would wait to see the people's reaction when they would see the chickens staggering around the yard with their wings flapping and nobody could understand what was the matter with the chickens.

We would also go around the village collecting jam jars which we could sell for two pence each. We would then go over to O'Brien's store and the clerk would count the jars and give us two pence for each one and he would say "OK – bring them in the back and put them in the boxes outside in the yard." We would get our money and we would walk out the back door but we wouldn't put the jam jars down – we would keep right on going. We would hide the jars and a week later we would go back and sell them to him again. We would do that often so we could buy candy.

We also would steal apples from everyone's apple trees. We had about fifteen apple trees at our house but we thought the other apples tasted better and it was more fun. We were kids looking for something to do.

One day we decided we were going to build a plough and use our dogs to pull it to cultivate the garden. Everything went fine until we harnessed the dogs together with rope. Obviously the dogs didn't appreciate our idea because they immediately attacked each other. It took several of our neighbors to separate them before they killed one another. Needless to say, that ended our experiment.

We really believed life was good – there was only one phone in the village and that was in the Post Office -- there was no electricity – no radios – certainly there was no television but we had fun doing what we called rambling. We would go to each other's house and sit around the fire and see who could tell the biggest lies or who could tell the best ghost story. Sometimes they were so scary that afterwards we were afraid to go out in the dark to go home.

My mom was a very hard working lady. She primarily ran the business and Mary; our live-in-maid took care of the children and helped with the housework. Dad did not enjoy working in the store -- he really liked running the farm.

The winters in Ireland were difficult – daylight was from approximately nine in the morning to four in the evening. The climate was wet, cold and miserable. In summer the sun would rise about three in the morning and we would still be playing ball at eleven at night and it was still daylight. There was a very short period of darkness.

The weather was not conducive to bicycle riding but we had to ride our bikes three miles each way to school every day. Often by the time we arrived, we would be soaking wet and freezing cold and had to sit in a classroom that was warmed only by a peat fire. We were very lucky to have a teacher who was really wonderful. It was a one-room school house and she taught all the classes from Kindergarten to sixth grade. She was a very kind, caring person. Miss Bridie O'Beirne lived with her sister and her husband on the other side of the fence from our farm. She knew our family all her life.

The school was part of a domain that was owned by a family named Cameron, who was English gentry. When England ruled Ireland, they gave their English families huge tracts of land and they built mansions on them. The school was part of their property and was used to educate the children of their servants.

When Ireland got its independence they confiscated those lands and the Irish Government divided the lands and distributed them among small Irish farmers. The school became the property of the Irish Government and became a public school. That is the building I went to school in.

The Cameron family remained living in the house after their land was confiscated and were still living there while I attended school. Some years later the family moved out and the contents of the house were auctioned. I attended that auction with my mom. Afterwards those beautiful buildings were burned to the ground.

The school was situated in dense woods and the main house or mansion was about a half mile deeper into the woods and they had all kinds of exotic birds and animals – actually it was more like a zoo. It was an incredible location.

Each morning a pupil would be assigned the task of getting a pail of water from the well located adjacent to the main residence. You attached the pail to the end of a rope and lowered it into the water and you turned the handle to raise it to the surface. You would start out with a full pail and when you arrived at the school you usually would have spilled half of it.

One stormy day there were high winds and torrential rain. Chris and I were riding our bicycles home and I was wearing a waterproof cape. It had no sleeves but went over your shoulders and covered your arms and even went over the handlebars on your bicycle. Only your legs and feet got soaked but the rest of you stayed pretty dry.

We were traveling at a high speed, assisted by the winds, when suddenly a gust of wind got under my cape, blowing it over my head cutting off my vision. I slammed into a wall and it was a miracle that I wasn't killed. Somehow I came out of it alright – apparently I was knocked out for a few minutes but I came to and got back on the bicycle -- I had no choice and headed home. That was the worst experience I had on my bicycle traveling to school.

There was a little boy attending school with his older sister and I believe he was in first grade. When the weather was bad I always put him on my bicycle and would drop him off at his house. He lived about two miles from the school. I don't know why he wasn't on the bike that day but I was so glad he wasn't because he probably would have been killed.

CHAPTER 2

One of the highlights of my childhood was the Blacksmith Shop in our yard. The blacksmith's name was George Coyle and his brother Joe was his helper. They did all kinds of work. They made horseshoes, shoed horses; fixed all kinds of farm equipment, lawn mowers, anything that had to do with ironwork and it was also the local social club. People would stop in and shoot the breeze. It was a great stop off place particularly in the winter because it was a nice warm place to congregate.

The iron was heated on a bed of coal and air from a hand operated bellows was forced through it to produce the necessary high temperatures. The goal of every child in the village was to be tall enough to reach the bellows handle and pump it up and down.

A lot of adults would go in and stand around and chat with Joe and George while the iron was being heated. George would remove the heated iron from the fire and bring it to the anvil and shape it into the necessary form. It was very interesting to watch. The farmers brought their horses there to be shod. There would be great excitement when the young horses were being shod for the first time – they would kick and scream and we thought it was hilarious to watch.

Joe and George were really nice men. Many a pleasurable hour of my childhood was spent looking at them working and listening to their stories. It was quite a place and I have some very fond memories of being there.

Every morning the fire in the blacksmith shop had to be relit and Joe would come into our kitchen with a metal pan to carry a lit sod of turf from our kitchen fire. From this they would light their fire in the forge. This routine went on everyday – I can still visualize Joe going off with a lit sod of turf in his little pan.

Speaking of turf – or another word for it is peat – that's what our homes were heated with. It was abundant in Ireland and coal was extremely expensive so practically everybody heated their homes with a turf fire.

Turf is an accumulation of partially decayed vegetation matter – an early form of coal. Peat bogs in Ireland are cool, wet, dark and slightly acidic. This alters the affect of bacteria and fungi so that materials in bogs decay very slowly.

Turf has to be cut into a sod which is slightly larger than a brick and is cut with a tool called a sleane (turf spade) which is similar to an L shaped spade. It is cut one sod at a time and it is put onto wagons and wheeled out onto the surface where it is spread out to dry. The time needed for this depends on weather conditions. This has to be done every year because you have to cut enough turf to last you through the year so it was a major, major undertaking.

You spent days just cutting it and after it partially dried, it was turned over so the other side could dry and that was how we kept our homes warm and did our cooking. It was a lot of work but turf was a very necessary part of our lives.

Everybody congregated around the fire – it was their source of heat and comfort. Even when the bar would close – which was around ten o'clock – many of the bar patrons would come to our kitchen and would sit around the fire and talk, and talk and talk. I guess that's what they mean when they say the Irish have a great gift of the gab because that was the only entertainment they had and they really loved to talk. They did not know how to go home and go to bed. Going to bed really wasn't important and getting up wasn't high on their agenda either. That was the way their life was.

There were 6 fireplaces in our house. Four were in the living quarters, one in the bar and one in the grocery store. The only active one in the living quarters was the kitchen fireplace and that was the only source of heat that we had throughout the house because Mom said that one time during a very cold spell she lit fires in the sleeping areas upstairs and the next morning everyone in the house had a bad cold. That was the end of the fires in the sleeping areas so the only active fireplace was in the kitchen. All the cooking was done there, all the hot water had to be heated there and it was kind of a busy place.

Every Wednesday was designated as "Wash Day" – the day all the clothing in the house was washed. Of course all the water had to be boiled and then poured into a big wash tub with a wash board in it. Soap came in large bars so they would have to place the bars in hot water to dissolve and then pour the liquid into the hot water in the tub. They had to scrub each piece of clothing on the washboard to get it clean. It was a major responsibility – an all day job by the time they boiled the water to wash the clothing – got it all clean and boil the water to rinse the clothing – this went on for hours and hours.

In the winter everybody practically lived in the kitchen because that was the only place that was warm. When you went to bed at night you got undressed and into bed in a big hurry because the bedrooms were really cold.

Our main source of lighting was from kerosene lamps and candles. We had no electricity so when you were going to bed at night, you had a candle in a candlestick and when you walked, because of the drafts; you had to cup the candle in the palm of your hand to keep the wind from extinguishing the candle. Houses were rather drafty because they were not sealed well. A gust of wind was enough to blow out the candle if you walked fast through the house.

Of course, every evening the kerosene lamps had to be filled so that was another chore. Someone was assigned that job and another one was assigned the job of bringing in sufficient turf to keep the fire going so we all had our own little chores.

One day a week would be Bottling Day in the bar. Maureen, Chris and I would help with the washing and scrubbing of hundreds of empty Guinness Stout bottles. Then after they were properly rinsed and drained, we would fill each bottle from the keg. The corks would be boiled to soften them – and then they would be inserted into each bottle and driven in with a wooden mallet. When that was completed, each bottle had to be labeled and stacked. This wasn't one of our more popular days.

After school I would have to go to the garden to dig the potatoes for dinner and mom would tell me what other vegetables she needed. We grew potatoes, cabbage, onions, carrots, celery, scallions, rhubarb, radishes, strawberries, gooseberries and of course apples. We had a lot of apple trees that produced different varieties. I would pick, dig or pull whatever we needed and bring them in and wash them so mom could get our dinner ready. It beat going to the grocery store. The thing I disliked the most was weeding the garden – you were on your knees for hours in the hot sun, pulling each weed from around whatever was planted. All I wanted to do was play ball or go swimming in the River Shannon.

Apple pies were very popular and homemade apple sauce with custard was a favorite dessert. That is probably the reason that today I really dislike apple pie or apple sauce because I probably had too much of it as a child.

So the three oldest ones really had our chores lined up for us between going to the well to get the water and going to bring in the turf – putting kerosene in the lamps and cleaning the chimneys as well as trimming the wicks on the lamp so they wouldn't smoke up and blacken the chimneys.

Maureen very often helped out in the bar and Christine would work in the grocery store and I didn't like either of those two chores so I would get other jobs to do.

Those were the assignments around home but we also had little jobs when it came to the farm - particularly in late fall and winter and early spring.

We usually had four milking cows and anywhere from four to six calves aging from very young to young, that had to be housed in the cold weather. Each evening we would go to the farm, which was about a mile from the house, and we could either walk or ride our bike and get the four cows and however many calves we had and walk them home with the help of our sheep dog and put them into their stables. That was one of the big chores that had to be done daily. My dad would walk them to the farm in the morning but they would have to be brought back every evening to be bedded down.

The cows had to be milked and that was a major chore to milk four cows and was not a fun experience. It was time consuming and tiring.

Cows got milked morning and evening seven days a week. The milk was then taken into the dairy room where it was strained into containers and left to cool. When the milk would cool down, the cream would rise and float on the top of the milk -- the cream would then be skimmed off the milk and put into another container.

About once a week the cream would be churned into butter. The churn consisted of a round wooden container with a tight lid on top. The handle was connected to paddles inside the churn and that agitated the cream when you turned the handle and you had to keep it going rather fast and continue doing so for a long time.

When one of us got tired, someone else would take over and we would keep it going until the cream turned into butter, which would float on the surface of the milk. After the butter was removed, whatever milk remained would be buttermilk. The butter was then shaped into squares of about a pound in weight and wrapped and stored away.

The original milk that was there before the cream was taken off, was the milk we used in the house for tea, coffee or whatever milk was needed for and what wasn't used was taken and put into pails and was fed to the baby calves. That is what the baby calves got for their meals. The very young baby calves had a problem because they were separated from their mother immediately after birth so they never had the opportunity to suck from their mother's nipple and they didn't know how to drink.

The only thing they knew was how to suck so when you brought the milk out in a pail, you had to take the baby calf and put your fingers in his mouth which he would start sucking. Then you would lower his head and your fingers down into the milk and as he was sucking on your fingers he would get the milk that way. That was a funny operation – their tongue always felt like wet sandpaper, but that was how you taught them how to drink. That pretty much sums up what a normal, routine day was in our lives when we were growing up. It was a very diversified way of life.

We didn't work all the time, we did have some time to play games like football or tag ball or whatever interested us. In addition to that, we had school work that had to be completed and that was pretty much life as I remember it.

CHAPTER 3

On that beautiful summer's morning of June 27, 1939, there was little to indicate the tragedy that was about to occur that would change my life and the lives of my family forever. Little did I know when my dad spoke to me before I left for school that morning that this would be the last time I would ever hear his voice. Within two hours, he was dead from a massive brain aneurysm.

My sister, Chris, and I were on our way home from school that afternoon when Joe Coyle, the blacksmith, met us about a mile from the house. We were surprised to see him because he should have been at work at the forge. He told us that Dad was very sick and he just wanted us to know. I said, "Gee he was fine this morning when we were leaving for school" and he told us that he became sick after we left.

We were shocked at this news and we got back on our bikes and continued on home and when we arrived at the house, we were surprised to see the store locked up and the hall door going to our living quarters was wide open. Mom met us in the hallway and we asked her how dad was and she said, "He is dead." I said, "Oh my God, he can't be, I was just talking to him before I left for school." She said, "I know, I know." I thought the world collapsed on top of me. I thought this can't be happening.

I cried and I sobbed and I sobbed and cried some more and everyone around me was sobbing and I couldn't comprehend what was happening. Dad was only 49-years-old. My dad was waked in the upstairs bedroom and people kept coming in droves and I was in a complete daze. I didn't know what to do or what to say. I would go into the room and sit and stare at his body – I kept staring at him and thinking that he is not dead and if I keep staring at him, his face will move. I just thought if I watched very carefully, I would see his eyes open – please God, let it happen.

I resented all those people and I wished they would just stop talking and if one more person said, "You know, Malachy, you are the Man of the House now" I would scream. I just couldn't take it anymore. Stop, I am not the man of anything – I am an 11-year-old kid. I couldn't believe what was happening – I was in a total daze and when the wake was finally over, they put his body into a coffin and it was taken to the Church. The next morning they had a Funeral Mass and after the Mass he was taken to the Graveyard in Roscommon and buried. I wouldn't go to the Graveyard – I couldn't bear to see him buried – I just wanted to be alone.

During this period, Mom called me into a quiet room and said, "Malachy, there is nobody to look after the livestock on the farm. The cows have to be milked, the calves have to be fed, the pigs have to be fed and I have no one to do it. Would you take care of the chores? Nobody has been up on the farm to check on the cattle and the sheep and to see if everything is OK". This was my first lesson that life goes on – even in death. That was the first of many lessons I was to learn in a short while.

One of the first things I became aware of was how unpleasant it is to be the oldest boy in a family where the father suddenly died. My oldest sister, Maureen, was in high school in the Convent of Mercy in Roscommon and my next sister, Chris, was in grammar school with me in Mount Plunkett. The next oldest boy was Kevin, who was two years younger than me followed by Eamon, Catherine, John and Anita. Anita was only a year and a half at the time. Talk about being in the wrong place at the wrong time – that was me. The only one in a worse spot was my mom – what a horrible position to be in at forty-four years of age, to be responsible for a bar, a grocery store, a farm of seventy acres, eight living children – ranging in age from one and a half to fourteen years old and I am pretty sure not too much cash available.

Ireland in the 30s, like a lot of other countries, was not in great financial shape. Property-wise, we were rich. Cash-wise, we were poor. To find anyone with work experience was almost impossible. However, one little thing in mom's favor was the time of year because the livestock pretty much roamed free, just grazing outdoors and you didn't have to bed them down. Instead of having to go up to the farm to get the cows and calves like you do in the fall and winter, in the summer you can go to the farm and milk the cows and the little calves could be kept close to home.

Also affected was my best friend, Malachy Murray. Malachy would come over to our house for me to go out and play and I couldn't go because I had too many things to do around home and as a result we saw less and less of each other. But we remained best friends. He would come over to visit often and a few months after dad died, Malachy's mom told me he was sick and they had to take him to the hospital.

A few days later he died. He died from what they called Infantile Paralysis – later known as Polio. So, in a few months, I lost my dad and my very best friend. I kept wondering what was going to happen next.

CHAPTER 4

I didn't have long to wait because on Sept. 1, Nazi Germany invaded Poland, which was the start of WWII. War was declared on Sept. 1, 1939. Little did I know what an effect this was going to have on my family. How could a war between Germany and Poland effect Ireland? The first thing that Ireland did was to declare to the world that it was a neutral country –so being neutral in a World War rightfully has a price to be paid.

The price was that there were practically no imports or exports – which made it very difficult for a little island like Ireland to support and feed itself. Without imports from abroad, we were going to have to produce everything ourselves. The government decided to survey every farm in Ireland to determine what land was capable of producing crops. They called it "arable land." Then they decided that a percentage of that must be cultivated – in our case that was twenty one acres. They also determined how many acres of that must be planted with wheat and I cannot remember how many acres that amounted to but the remainder of the twenty one acres could be planted with crops of your choice but it had to be planted. If you didn't comply, the government would confiscate your farm.

This was like a bombshell. How in heaven's name were we going to be able to comply with this directive? The government would take our farm, we didn't have anybody that could plough and cultivate twenty one acres. I said, "Mom, we are not going to lose our farm because I will do it." She said, "You, what do you know about ploughing?" I said, "I know enough to know that I can handle it."

I had been with dad when he was ploughing so I knew what it was about and I had been around horses since I have been able to walk but we did have a problem at this time because we only had one horse. We would have to buy another one. I was pretty big and I was pretty strong and I knew I could learn. Anyhow we didn't have to worry about that until next winter which would give us time to get a horse. And mom said, "Who is going to do that?" I replied, "I know I can."

She had a lot of doubts about it but she didn't have many choices. On Nov. 3 at the horse fair in the town of Athlone, we bought a beautiful 18-month-old mare. This was the normal age to buy a horse that you wanted to train. Dad had a very good selection of farm equipment and the only thing lacking was a second horse. This was the first major decision resolved, at least in theory.

I brought the horse home and took the halter off her and let her loose in the stable and the next morning I went back to the stable and opened the door to put the halter back on her. She took one look at me, pulled her ears back, bared her teeth and let out a scream and charged at me. I saw her coming and backed out of the door and slammed it. She scared the hell out of me.

Now I had a big problem. How was I going to put a halter on this crazy horse? This was a major problem since I was the guy who told his mother that he would train this horse and here he couldn't even put the halter on her. I knew I had to do something but what? I thought maybe there would be someone in the bar that could help me.

It was my lucky day, Ned Foley was there and he was a very nice guy. I whispered my problem into his ear and he listened very sincerely and he smiled and said, "Let me give you a little advice on how to handle a horse. Never, but never, let a horse sense that you are afraid because a horse can sense fear. Come and let me show you." We went to the stable and opened the door. He walked right in and he waved his arm with the halter and spoke real loud and the next thing I knew the horse was in the corner shaking with fear. That was the best lesson I think I ever learned. It was true and it helped me many times over the years.

Now that I had the halter on her, the breaking-in would start. Of course, the first thing I wanted to do was get up on her and start riding. The only harness necessary for this was a halter and reins. I didn't own a saddle and even if I did, I wouldn't know what to do with it as I had never ridden with one – the only way I knew how to ride was bareback. Here we had a wild horse that didn't even want a human to put their hands on her, never mind having someone stupid enough to think they were going to get up on her back and ride her. She didn't appreciate my putting my hands across her back, let alone putting any part of my body on her.

I soon learned how fast she could leap and turn and twist those hind legs. She was determined that I wasn't going to ride her and I was equally determined that I was and the war of the wits was on. When I finally did manage to get up on her back, immediately I was looking down on the world from a whole different perspective. She reared up on her hind legs and danced around with my legs clamped around her belly. I am sure the view was great from up there but I didn't appreciate it because the next instant I was viewing the ground from a whole new angle.

Kitty (the name I called her) changed positions going from her hind legs to her front ones so swiftly that I thought that my head had snapped from my neck. This was repeated over and over with slight variations enough to give me views from the horse's underside. I got trampled on, kicked and bitten and then she gave sudden bursts of forward motion followed with sudden stops. The only problem with this was that sometimes you kept going without the horse. Occasionally you managed to stop when she did and eventually this all stopped for no apparent reason.

It was almost like she became exhausted, thought it over and figured it was not worth fighting over. She became a whole new animal and became my favorite and I loved to ride her. Next came her introduction to being harnessed in order to pull a wagon for ploughing and all the things that were to follow. She did act up sometimes but all in all she settled in with much less disagreement. That was one problem kind of solved but the next one might not get solved quite as easily.

At least the horse had me to break her in but who was going to do this for me? There was no one and now I wondered if I could keep my promise to my mom that I was so cocky in making. The very first thing you must learn in the field that you are going to plough was that it had to be laid out so that eventually the two lines would come together and it must be precise. When you decided where you were going to start, you had to set up markers and they must be absolutely straight. If the field is seven hundred or eight hundred feet long, you would have to put a marker every fifty feet. You started out with one marker at each end of the field and then my sister Maureen would come and help me. I would lay on the ground and sight from the first marker to the one at the other end of the field and she would add each marker as I sighted down the line and when she would come into my view, I would signal where to put the marker. The end result was a perfectly straight line.

With that job done, the next job was to get the horses to walk that line and at the same time try and control the plough. It wasn't easy but it could be done and the more you did it, the easier it became. Now I had harnessed the team of horses to the plough. This was the moment of truth –"Dear God, help us" was all I could say and He did and everything went exceptionally well. Day after day, we kept going and finally the whole twenty one acres was ploughed and finished so the Department of Agriculture was off our backs.

In about six weeks time, we were ready to plant and once again I had never done this either. Wheat, oats and barley had to be planted. I don't remember the exact percentage of wheat that had to be planted but I would guess that it was between five and six acres. We usually planted about an acre of potatoes and maybe a quarter of an acre of turnips and mangles (a vegetable, similar to a turnip that we used to feed the livestock) and the remainder would be mostly oats and barley. The planting of wheat, barley and oats didn't consume a lot of time – in fact I was able to get that finished in a few days but the potatoes, mangles and turnips were much more time consuming.

The soil needed much more cultivating and it would be done using drills. This required a special type of plough. This plough would make a deep V in the soil pushing the soil to each side of it. Then the next V would be next to that so it would end with a point, then a valley, then another point and a valley and so on and on. Then you carted the fertilizer from the stables and spread it in the valleys. You then took a piece of a potato that had at least one eye or maybe two and planted them one foot apart one after another on top of the fertilizer. You did this row after row, then you took the horses and the plough – the same plough that was used to make the drills and run the plough in the middle of the peak which would then become the valley and the valley would become the peak. The potatoes would then be planted and we'd be finished with them. The same method was used for the turnips and the mangles, except that a special machine was used for planting the seeds.

When the wheat, oats and barley were spread on the soil, you had to harness the horses to a harrow – a device with many teeth in it and it would spread the soil over the seeds. Then you followed with a heavy roller about six feet long which would also help to cover the seeds.

Each morning the day started with the feeding of the horses. You gave them hay and oats – horses love oats. They were going to have a hard day's work ahead of them and they must be well cared for. The cows had to be milked and the calves must be fed. The cows need not be fed after milking in the morning because they are going out to pasture. Someone had to feed the pigs. My main interest was the horses. I would put oats into a small bag and hang it on their harness and that would be their lunch. After the cows were milked and the calves fed and I had my breakfast, I would take them to the farm. This would be the routine in the early spring.

Later on in the summer, the cows would remain out on the farm and milked there. This time of year I would seldom be asked about milking the cows or feeding the pigs or anything like that because I had more than I could take care of with the livestock on the farm, which were my problem. Also I had to check everyday to see that they were all there. The sheep got themselves into trouble constantly. Their wool would get caught in the bushes and briars and they could die there from strangulation if you didn't find them. If you found that one was missing you would have to find him or her and pull it free.

When the sheep were having their babies, usually in late Feb. or early March, you would check them every evening about eleven o'clock. By then it was pitch black so you would have to use a powerful carbide lamp and walk all around the field and find any ewe that was giving birth. You would always find her far away from all the others by herself and then you would help her with the birth. The lamp was the only source of light. Sometimes you would have two or three giving birth all in one night.

You got pretty good helping to deliver and sometimes the baby would be coming out turned in the wrong direction and you would have your arm halfway inside the mother and turn the baby around. You would have to go and check them again about six in the morning. During this period you didn't get much sleep. As dawn arrived I would return home and have my breakfast and go to school. That night the process would be repeated all over again. This would go on until all 80 or 90 ewes had their babies.

Later on when the weather got warmer and the flies came out, they would lay their eggs on the backs of the sheep in their wool and the eggs hatched out and the little white maggots would appear by the hundreds and they would feed on the flesh of the sheep. You usually could tell which was infected but each day all of them would have to be rounded up into a pen and you would have to check each one and on the infected ones you had to put disinfectant to kill the maggots and rub them out of the wool. During the summer you had to go through this routine everyday – just one more thing to be done daily.

During all this time mom was trying to hire someone to work but there wasn't anybody available. All the available men had left the country and went to England where there was a huge shortage of manpower. All their manpower was in the armed forces and they needed people to work in the factories and the pay was so much better than it was in Ireland, making it just about impossible to find anybody. Eventually she found a man, who could be my grandfather. He was a nice person who loved to talk and talk but wasn't interested in work. However, he did pick up a lot of the chores which made life a little easier for everyone.

At that time, my sister Maureen went to England and became a nurse. She was on duty one night at the hospital in the city of Bath when the German Luftwaffe came in over the city and wave after wave of planes dropped their bombs and then they flew over the rooftops and machine gunned the streets. The hospital wasn't hit. Many of the young Irish joined the British Armed Forces. As a result, laborers just didn't exist.

The effect of the war seemed endless – most food was either rationed or just didn't exist, for instance tea was rationed at a half-ounce per person per week. Butter, sugar and white bread disappeared totally and it was replaced with black bread. It was so heavy and so horrible you couldn't eat it. A two pound loaf was only about the size of a brick.

All private cars were banned from the roads. Gas was only available for emergency vehicles and trains were cut down to one a day. You could only return the next day. There were no rubber imports so if your bike blew a tire, you couldn't replace it. Candles were almost impossible to get so the only thing we could get sometimes was kerosene. We had to make our own candles from fat. Tobacco of all kinds was next to impossible to get and the list goes on and on. Your world shrunk down to a distance of a few miles. If you didn't have a working bicycle, you had to walk so you didn't travel far from home.

Now, after all the plowing and the planting, we just had to wait to see the results. When the first signs of life appeared above ground, it was a fantastic feeling. Well, now it was summer and the weather was getting warm. The hay had to be cut and saved. Hay comes from grass that is left to grow to at least a foot high. It was then cut with a mower and left in the sun to dry. Sunshine was essential for this operation and Ireland didn't get too much of it. The sun dried the grass changing it to hay, which could then be stored for food, so the animals could feed for the winter months.

Even the sheep and the cattle that live outdoors all year round need hay. There was not enough grass in the winter for them to survive. Depending on how good the weather was would determine if it was a long or a short process. The hay must be completely dry before storing – you couldn't store it damp or wet.

Once or twice during the summer the sheep had to be rounded up and taken to be dipped in a chemical. This gave the sheep some protection against the flies laying eggs in their wool. The summers were a rather nice time. Everything had been planted and the hay had been taken care of. School was out and the two horses were out to pasture and actually putting on weight. They deserved a little vacation.

One morning one of them jumped a fence into a pasture where she shouldn't have been. I went in after her and thought, "Ok, you jumped the fence to get in, you can jump the fence to get out again." I jumped up on her back with no halter or anything and gave her a good slap. She took off at a gallop. We went around the field and headed towards the fence and I hit her on the side of the head in the direction I wanted her to go. Now she was headed for the fence at a gallop and just as she got close to it, she suddenly stopped and I wasn't expecting that. I went flying out between her ears and over the fence and hit the ground like a ton of bricks. I was out and she was still in so I had to go back and start all over again but this time I used the gate, which is probably what I should have done in the first place.

During this lull, I actually got a chance to go swimming in the River Shannon. In the meantime, the wheat, oats and barley had grown several inches and I couldn't believe how beautiful it looked. I had no idea it would be so perfect. I didn't know if I had under-seeded or over-seeded and after all the unknowns I was absolutely shocked. For the first time I felt there was hope for survival – if we made it through this, we should make it through the harvest OK.

When harvest came we were very fortunate, the weather remained nice. The rain stayed away and several friends and neighbors came to help. When the wheat, oats and barley ripened you had a very short time to get it harvested, otherwise the kernels fell to the ground and were lost.

When that happened, what was left turned to straw and that had little value. The short reprieve that we had didn't last very long – all those corn crops, including the hay had to be gathered up and brought to the haggard to be stored. Then the wheat, oats and barley had to be thrashed – that means the kernels were separated from the straw. The straw was used for bedding for the animals and the kernels were ground into flour, oatmeal and whatever. This was the final result of all the work. One acre of potatoes had to be dug out of the ground by hand and stored as well as the mangles and turnips. Then the turf had to be carted from the bog and this took about a week of time. When all that was completed, you were pretty well prepared for the winter.

By early Oct. the weather usually turned very cold and the winters were very windy and stormy. We would get a lot of frost and some snow and every once in a while we would get a major snow fall. All major work on the farm ended and then it was routine caring for the animals. Basically this was life during the first year of World War II in Ireland as I remember it; and with a few minor variations the same routine continued for the next six years.

The plus side of all this was that when the farmer complied with the government's demands he was free to sell his products on the open market. This was a big help financially for your family.

The day that the war ended was a very exciting day. The only one that was almost equal in excitement was the day that I saw my first loaf of white bread. Life for everyone started to return to normal but it didn't change overnight. Actually it took a few years to get anywhere near normal for us. It took that long to get all the land that was cultivated to return to pasture and to increase the livestock for grazing but at least the pressures were relieved. No more quotas to be met. You could go to school, play ball, go for a swim and do all the things you couldn't do before.

During this period, my Uncle Mike Gately returned from the States for a visit. He was my mom's brother and he came over with his wife, Aunt Mary, and their two sons, Michael and Timmy, and their daughter June. They even brought their car over by ship. They arrived one day during sheep sheering time. They were fascinated to see all the wool everywhere and to see the sheep being branded. They thought that was the greatest.

During that time my uncle asked me if I ever considered going to the States. He said, "You know you are a U.S. citizen and you can go there anytime you want to." I said, "I know but I haven't had any time to even think about it." He said, "If you ever want to come, I will send you a ticket and you can pay me back anytime." I had never really thought about it before but once it was brought to my attention, I became very interested. Many times I had thought about disappearing and getting away from this crazy place I found myself in but I couldn't do this to mom and my sisters and brothers. They needed me but now they were older and the war was long over.

CHAPTER 5

I have no recollection of how I approached mom but I do remember going to Dublin, to the American Consulate and filling out an application for a passport. When the passport was issued it was valid for ninety days. The letter that accompanied it told me that I had "ninety days to go home."

The next thing I remember was my mother and my Uncle Pat Donoghue driving me to Shannon Airport. I draw a complete blank – I remember nothing about leaving home but at the airport Mom gave me a big hug and whispered, "I know you will be back within six months." To this day I feel like I abandoned her. We had been through so much together.

The only money I was allowed to take out of Ireland was one pound, which was the equivalent of five American dollars at that time and my total belongings were in one leather suitcase. We had a stopover in Gander, New Foundland, and I purchased something at the airport. I cashed my five dollar bill and got change in four Canadian dollars and some coins that I didn't understand because I was not familiar with the currency. So I landed on American soil on Feb. 19, 1949 with four Canadian dollars and some change. Many times I reminded my children that I came to the U.S. with less than five dollars to my name. So forever after I always felt that if I owned more than five dollars, I was ahead financially.

Forty years later, our daughter, Maura, went with some college friends to Russia during spring break. On their return trip their plane landed in Gander, New Foundland and Maura picked up a five dollar Canadian coin and when she returned home, she handed me the coin and said, "Here, Dad, here's the money you left in Canada on your first trip there – now we won't have to hear about it any more." So much for sympathy, I guess.

My plane landed at LaGuardia Airport. Kennedy airport, which was originally known as Idlewild Airport, didn't exist then. Customs came aboard the plane to check passports and when they approached me, they saw my place of birth was Ireland and they wanted to know how I was in possession of a U.S. Passport when I wasn't born here.

Everyone left the plane except me. They escorted me off the plane into a room and sat me down and started asking all kinds of questions. They just didn't understand this at all. Eventually I said to them, "If you have a problem with this, why don't you call Washington and ask them to explain it to you. They are the people that issued the passport and I am sure they knew what they were doing." They gave that some thought for a minute or two and then they released me. It wasn't a very warm reception to the U.S. Very few people entered the U.S. during the war years. I arrived on Feb. 19, 1949, and obviously they weren't familiar with cases like mine.

Uncle Mike and Aunt Mary Gately were there to greet me and drove me to their home on Rowland Street in the Bronx. That night was my first experience sleeping in a house with heat. I could not understand why they needed it.

The next day was Sunday and in the morning we all went to church. We attended St. Raymond's Church on Tremont Avenue and I was amazed at the size of the church. I thought I was in a cathedral.

Later that day I wrote a letter to Mom telling her that I had arrived safely. Back then you just didn't pick up the phone and call home. A three minute call to Ireland was $55 so instead you sent an airmail letter which would arrive a week or ten days later.

When I finished the letter I must have gotten a stamp from someone. I asked Uncle Mike where I could mail it. He said, "Just go out the front door, turn left and walk to the first street corner and there you will see a tall red box with a handle on it. It will say 'Pull Here' and when you do that you put the letter in." I walked to the corner and read what was said on it – "Fire Alarm Box: For Emergency Use Only." I didn't deposit the letter, I put it in my pocket and came back to the house and said nothing. He asked me if I had mailed the letter and I said I did. That puzzled him but he didn't ask for an explanation. In any event the fire engines didn't come roaring down the street.

A few months later I was watching TV and an ad came on for some furniture store advertising three rooms of furniture for some low price. I called them up and introduced myself as Mike Gately and gave his address on Rowland Street in the Bronx and ordered the furniture and said the payment would be made on delivery. Of course, I never heard the outcome and I never inquired either. I figured one good turn deserved another.

My Uncle Mike told me he had made a lot of inquiries about a job for me and there just weren't any jobs available. What made it so difficult was that the troops were still returning from the war and there were no jobs for them. He suggested that I go to work for him in one of his bars as a bartender. He had a bar on Zerega Avenue which I could walk to from his house. I needed a job but working in a bar was definitely not my favorite choice. I didn't want to work in our bar in Ireland or any other bar but this was where I was going to end up.

He told me, "For this, I will pay you $35 a week. Your hours will be eight in the morning to five in the evening Monday through Saturday and noon to five o'clock on Sunday. You can continue to live at our house and the rent will be $15 a week." He also said he had to deduct for Social Security and later on I realized he couldn't take out for Social Security because I didn't have a Social Security card or number. I agreed to this arrangement as I really had no choice because I needed a job and I became a bartender. I must have learned the currency pretty fast because I wouldn't have survived if I hadn't.

Things went OK. I had to learn to mix drinks and make all kinds of cocktails. I wasn't an expert but I managed. The most difficult part of the job was having to listen to everyone's problems. The women cried on your shoulder about their husbands, boyfriends and lovers - and very often you had heard the same story from their boyfriends and husbands the day before. You couldn't believe some of the stories you were hearing and sometimes you had to give them a tissue to wipe away their tears. Why someone would discuss those things with a bartender I could never comprehend. Then, when I had a problem, I didn't have a person I could discuss it with.

At five o'clock, Uncle Mike was scheduled to relieve me. He would arrive at the bar around five o'clock but then he would sit at the bar and buy everyone a round of drinks, which I would serve. He would talk to the customers for at least a half hour and I couldn't leave until such time as he would put on his apron and come behind the bar. If I got out by six o'clock, I would consider myself very lucky.

I would then walk back to the house and most evenings I would take their terriers for a walk. They bred Irish terriers for show. They had one dog that had taken first prize at Madison Square Garden. His name was Stony Dysart, which was the name of the area in Ireland where my uncle was born. This dog was extremely valuable for breeding purposes. One day the dog just disappeared from their yard. Someone had to have stolen her because none of the other dogs were missing.

My Aunt Mary was inconsolable. She spent weeks crying on the phone with every agency in the city. The dog was never found. My Aunt Mary was very kind and I liked her very much. This was pretty much my routine every day and the weeks passed and all I had seen of New York was from their house to the bar, work everyday, then go home and walk the dogs, have dinner and go to bed. That was as much as I had done and after five weeks of this, I said to myself that there had to be more to life than this.

On the Saturday evening of the fifth week, Uncle Mike arrived as usual and he put on his apron as I was taking mine off. I rolled up my apron in a nice little ball and threw it at him and I said, "Keep your job" and I walked out. I walked back to the house and packed my bag and left. Now I found myself on the street with no idea of where I was or where I was going.

The only thing I remember was standing on the sidewalk outside a bar and it was very noisy inside and people were singing and I remember asking myself, what is there to sing about? That seemed to be the second time in my life that I had erased everything from my mind. To this day, I have no idea of where I went or what I did. No matter how hard I try to find the answer to that, I cannot come up with it.

I do remember that I had a total of $35 in assets after my five weeks work. I did have an address of a neighbor's son. His dad lived across the street from us in Ireland. I had never known his son because he had left Ireland before I was born. His name was Michael Owens. I must have called him because he was probably the only one I would have contacted but I don't know this for a fact, but someone must have helped me. The very next thing I remember is I was living in a room, in a fifth floor walkup on 152nd Street off Melrose Avenue in the Bronx.

The landlady's name was Mrs. Reinhardt, a German lady- a tough piece of work. I used to love to read and at 10 o'clock every night she would knock on my door and tell me to turn off the light as I was wasting electricity. The room had one ceiling lamp with a forty watt bulb. I paid her five dollars a week for the room.

Michael Owens turned out to be a very good friend and his wife was also very nice. He was an assistant manager for the AandP Company and he managed to get me a job working two days a week in the AandP. My pay for the two days was eighteen dollars so I paid five dollars out of that for the room and I ate my meals in restaurants. There wasn't any fast food around then. I went to a candy store for breakfast. A cup of coffee was 5 cents, a roll and butter was 10 cents, a telephone call was 5 cents, a subway ride was 5 cents and the Daily News was 2 cents.

I could get a very good dinner for 65 cents so I managed pretty well on my $18 and of course, I still had my $35 back-up. It's ironic that the very things I didn't want to do in Ireland, I ended up doing in New York. It just goes to prove that the grass is not always greener on the other side.

I cannot remember where the store was but it was a pleasant place to work. There weren't any openings for a full-time position. I put in an application in Safeway stores hoping a full-time position might come up and a short while later I received a call from them telling me they had a full-time position paying $42 a week for starters, going up to $57after the first year.

Around this time I decided to look up my father's two brothers and one lived on Teller Avenue in the Bronx. His name was Pete and the other uncle was Mickey who lived somewhere in Queens. I still hadn't met my mom's sister Marie and her husband Eugene McCarthy who lived in Brooklyn. Aunt Marie wasn't at all like my mom, she was rather stern but Uncle Eugene was very easy going. When I went to visit them, I stayed overnight and slept on their living room couch. I woke up sometime later and there was a girl standing over me asking, "Who are you?" I told her, "I am Malachy Donoghue" and she said, "Oh, you are my first cousin – I am your cousin Peggy."

Years later whenever I would meet her, she would always ask me "Who are you?" To this day she teases me like this whenever we meet. She was very nice – she had an older sister Maureen whose married name was Jenkins. I met her years later. Peggy had two brothers, Joe and Tommy, who were great guys.

Then I went to meet my father's brother, Pete, who was a New York City fireman. He was married to Aunt Mary and they had five children, three boys, Pete, Mickey and Eamon, and two girls, Anita and Betty. Anita was my favorite. She was absolutely beautiful and had a great sense of humor. Betty was very quiet and withdrawn. Anita and I would go to the movies and afterwards go to the candy store for ice cream and go for walks in the little park overlooking Yankee Stadium. Uncle Pete and Aunt Mary and their two older sons used to spend a lot of time in the local beer garden.

I met my dad's other brother, Uncle Mickey, and his wife, Aunt Evelyn, twice. They had five or six children whom I met for a few minutes. I really knew very little about them. He was also a New York City Fireman. As far as I knew, they were the only relatives I had here.

I was out walking one evening and I heard this heavy Northern Ireland accent and I went over to the fellow and asked him where he had come from. He said, "I came from County Monaghan and my name is John Daly." I introduced myself and told him I came from County Roscommon. He was the first young person that I had met from Ireland. He lived in the same area I did on Willis Avenue. We became great friends. My world was actually expanding.

Willis Avenue was the street on which my dad had owned a bar. It was on the corner of Willis Avenue and 140th Street. When dad returned to Ireland, he had left the bar to his brother Pat and mom's brother, Tom Gately. Later they also returned to Ireland and it was left to mom's brother, Mike. He owned it until 1947 and sold it and bought a bar in Rockaway Beach. The one on Zerega Avenue was where I had worked for him.

At this time Willis Avenue was practically all Irish and gradually Daly and I would meet any new arrivals. Paddy Briody arrived and later Frank Moekler and so on and so on. We looked forward to meeting anyone new in the area. There were also some Irish Dance Halls in Manhattan and we would go there every Saturday night. We would meet some Irish girls and then things started to get interesting.

During one of our "gab sessions" with the guys, I mentioned that my dad was in World War I and had worked here for many years. Someone asked if my mom had been entitled to V.A. benefits when my dad died and that got me thinking. I took myself down to the Veterans Administration Office and posed my question. They told me they would research it and a short while later my mother got the wonderful news that she would get a monthly check for herself and everyone under eighteen. What a tragedy that we didn't know this in 1939 when Dad died and all eight children were under that age and Mom could have used that money so desperately. However, it was a wonderful financial boost to mom and helped her so much. She was now able to send the girls to boarding schools and the money helped her purchase things she needed very badly.

My brother, Kevin, decided to come to the US and I went to meet him at the dock as he came by ship. When I got there my Aunt Marie was there also. Someone must have told her that he was coming, and it wasn't me. I thought he was coming with me but she decided otherwise, so we all ended up in Brooklyn.

Aunt Marie was a pretty determined lady. It seemed to me that she was accustomed to getting her way. I was just as determined that she wasn't going to succeed. As a result of that, I don't think I was ever one of her favorites. Kevin came to the Bronx and I had gotten him a room near where I was living. The next day we went to visit Uncle Pete and Aunt Mary Donoghue and we had dinner with them. Later Aunt Mary said that she was very good friends with the manager of the local Safeway store and she would ask him if he knew any manager that could give Kevin a job.

The next morning she spoke to the store manager and he said to have him come in to see him the next day as he would like to meet him. Aunt Mary picked Kevin up and took him to meet Mr. Campion, the store manager. Mr. Campion hired Kevin and he started working that day. He could walk to work. I had to travel by subway to the lower end of Manhattan, to Sixth Street and Avenue D.

Kevin really enjoyed the grocery business in Ireland so he was very happy to be working in Safeway. He and I got along very well as he was great company. Shortly after he started in Safeway, he didn't show up for work one day and didn't call the store to say that he was sick. Mr. Campion thought that was very strange that he didn't get word to him, so he went to his apartment. He found him very sick in bed. He was dehydrated, running a high fever and had nothing to eat. He got him out of bed and took him home to his house in a cab. They nursed him back to health and when he was well, he wouldn't hear of Kevin going back to that room. Kevin lived with the Campions the rest of the time he was in the U.S.

I had never met Mr. Campion, I only knew of him through Kevin. Then the Safeway stores had a company picnic on the 4th of July and it was there that I met the Campion family. The picnic was held at Tibbett's Brook in Westchester

County and that was where my meeting with Jerry Campion and his wife Mae and their son Ed and their two daughters, Maureen and Geraldine, took place. There was no way I could have known when I was introduced to Maureen in 1950 that I just met my future wife.

Mr. Campion never wanted to be called "Mr." He said his name was Jerry and that is how he was known. I thought they were a lovely family and we all had a great day. I became wonderful friends with them and spent many hours at their house. Shortly after, they found a nice place for me to move to just up the block from where they lived.

They had a very pretty home. It was a two family house with a lovely porch. They lived on the second floor and Jerry's aunt lived downstairs. It was on 175th St. facing Crotona Park in the Bronx. It was a beautiful park and a lovely setting.

Jerry was very active in St. Thomas Aquinas Church. He was a trustee of the church, and head of St. Vincent de Paul Society and Catholic Charities as well as running bingo. When he came home from work and had his dinner he would then go to the church for one thing or another. He was very involved and would get home very late. When the children were in bed, Mrs. Campion, Kevin and I would sit around the kitchen table and solve the world's problems.

Kevin and I had a lot of good times together. We went on boat rides up the Hudson River, and had some wild times down at Rockaway Beach, particularly on 103rd Street and we even dated two girls that were first cousins. He was very serious with his girl and I thought he might get married to her. We went to dances in the Jaeger House, the Leitrim House and the Caravan -- we visited them all. Did we ever have fun? Kevin was here for about a year and a half when we got a letter from Mom telling us that she really needed one of us to come home. She wasn't able to keep up with the work herself. I remember telling Kevin, "I don't know what you are going to do but I know one thing, I am not going back to Ireland." Kevin agreed to go as he really liked the grocery business. I was very sorry to see him leave and I really missed him.

After he left, I continued going to visit the Campions. I would help Jerry do some work around the house on weekends, plastering, painting, cutting the hedge in front of the house and when the heating system would have a problem we would work on that together. The three children were all in grammar school and Ed would have piano lessons on Saturday mornings in the convent, taught by one of the nuns.

I'll always remember one Saturday, Ed decided he was going skating instead of going to his piano lesson. On his way home from skating he passed the convent and who was standing in the doorway but the nun who was supposed to have given him his piano lesson. She grabbed one of the skates and hit him over the head with it. That was the end of Ed's piano playing.

Every student paid 50 cents for a lesson and Maureen tells the story that she took lessons once a week for a half-hour. When she got to her lesson the ninety year old nun, who was the piano teacher, would very often be asleep in her chair. The instructions were if she was asleep you dropped your 50 cents in the box and went into the kitchen and helped the sister working in there with the dishes. Not a bad deal – you paid for the privilege of washing dishes. Her parents were so proud when she played "Silent Night" at midnight Mass and I was there to witness her debut.

I used to ask Maureen her spelling words and years later I would remind her of the great spelling teacher that she had. To this day she says she is the better speller— and she is.

CHAPTER 6

I wasn't happy in New York City – the summers were unbearable with the heat and humidity and of course, there was no air conditioning in any of the apartments. I decided I'd like to move to California. I asked the Safeway store manager if I could get a transfer to a store in California and he said he didn't know but suggested that I put in a request, and he would see what he could do, which I did. A few weeks went by and one morning he told me that my request was granted and I had two weeks vacation coming to me. I could take my vacation and he gave me the name and address of the store and the manager that I was to report to, in San Diego. I was delighted.

My plan was that I would fly to Seattle, Washington, and I would have nearly two weeks to travel down the West Coast almost to the Mexican border. That would take care of my vacation. I booked a flight on an airline called ATA – American Transport Association. This was the strangest flight I have ever been on. It was like a Tramp Steamer that never knew where its next stop would be. It got so bad that when the stewardess made an announcement about where our next stop would be, she would add, "I hope so." One stop that I will always remember was somewhere in Montana and we had to disembark the plane. They didn't tell us why or for how long.

The plane stopped on the runway and you came down the ramp and when you looked out on each side of the runway there was a meadow with grass about twelve inches high and you had to walk through this grass to get to the terminal. It got so bad, it was actually funny.

I don't remember how many hours it took to get to Seattle, but I do know we arrived sometime during the night. I left New York to get away from the heat and humidity. When I arrived in Seattle it was much worse than where I had left. I guess I was weary and tired after the crazy flight I just came off and I sat down on a bench. There weren't many people in the airport – it was very quiet and I was sitting there sort of talking to myself and questioning my sanity. If it was this hot this far north, what would San Diego be like?

I said to myself, this is crazy. I walked over to the ticket counter and asked the girl if they had any flights going north. She said, "North to where?" I said, "I don't know – do you have flights going anywhere?" She mentioned that they had two flights going to Alaska – one to Anchorage and one to Fairbanks. Where did I want to go? I asked her where the first flight was going and she said Fairbanks, so I bought a ticket.

That night, I found myself on a Pan American flight and sitting next to me was a serviceman; an African-American man from the South. He had been home on leave and was returning to his outfit in Fairbanks. He wasn't exactly overjoyed. We landed in Fairbanks as the sun was rising. When we got to the terminal I asked this fellow if he would like a cup of coffee and he said he would love one.

We sat at the counter and were drinking our coffee when I was tapped on the shoulder. I turned around and there was a guy who said to me, "We don't do this kind of thing here." I didn't know what he was talking about and he turned and walked away. That was the only time I saw a sign of Jim Crow all the years I was in Alaska. As I was leaving the terminal, I was fascinated by a huge sign over the exit door that read, "Send not your foolish and feeble – send me your strong and sane." This is known as the Law of the Yukon.

I arrived in the city of Fairbanks and went into a restaurant to get breakfast. I was absolutely shocked at the prices. I could have had at least three breakfasts in New York for the price of a single breakfast there. As I sat at breakfast, I was thinking about the sign at the airport and it stirred something in me. For the first time in my life, I got a feeling that I cannot describe, but I felt like I was "free at last," free from everything that I had ever known and that I was home where I belonged. I walked around Fairbanks and felt like an idiot because I was wearing a suit and white shirt and tie, that was standard traveling clothes in those days but it definitely wasn't the standard in Alaska. There wasn't much I could do about it.

As I was strolling around there was a gentleman sitting on a bench and he said "Howdy, I see you are a stranger in town. Where did you come from?" I told him and he said sit down and we'll have a little chat. I sat down and he told me he was retired and where he had worked, and he wanted to know if I was going to stay in Alaska. I said that I hope to as long as I could find a job. He said, "I may be able to help you if you go to the FE Company." I asked him if that was the name of a company and he said it's Fairbanks Exploration actually and it's also known as The United States Smelting, Refining and Mining Company or USSR and M Company.

"It's a major gold mining company in the territory and I can tell you where their offices are located," he said. He wished me good luck. He gave me his name and address and said he was sure he would see me again. He did say you have to get rid of those clothes and if you get a job with them you will be in a camp somewhere - wherever they send you. You can put those clothes in your suitcase and I know a place here in town where you can store your luggage for as long as you want.

He gave me the name and address of the storage place. It was still early in the day so I went to the mining office and was hired on the spot. I was told to report to their office the next morning to go to camp. Now I had to move real fast. The first thing I had to do was get work clothes.

When I asked what I would need, I was told a sleeping bag, one pair of shoe packs, high wool socks, dungarees, a heavy shirt, work gloves and a work jacket. I had to shop for those items and be at their office ready for work at 8 am. The first thing I had to do was get rid of the leather suitcase and the suit and all the worldly possessions that I owned. All of this took place on the day I arrived.

I also had to find a place to stay that night so I wound up in the USO and asked to be woken up at 6 am. I had a cot in a dormitory setting. At 6 o'clock, I was being shaken and I rolled over and the first thing I saw was the handle of a Colt .45 sticking out of a holster. Did I wake up fast? That was one way to get people moving in the morning.

I arrived at the office before 8 am and climbed into a pickup truck that was headed for Gold Stream Camp about 12 miles north of Fairbanks. The guy who drove the pickup was very talkative and told me where he came from in the states. I asked him if he went back often and he answered that he had never gone back and he said he didn't intend to ever go back. He said he didn't think he could ever live there again. He then added, "Just wait, you will feel the same way in a very short time."

We finally arrived at the camp after passing some of the most beautiful wild flower areas I had ever seen. The buildings were all corrugated iron. The main structure was a large two story building. The upper floor was the sleeping quarters and the first floor was the mess hall and kitchen, all in one room. At the far end was the largest stove I had ever seen – it must have been 20 feet in length and the cooking and baking was all done there. The rest of the area consisted of about four rows of tables that ran the length of the room and on one side was a small table which was for the coffee pot and canned fruit which was there 24 hours a day. Any time you needed a snack, it was there waiting for you.

When we arrived, there was nobody to be seen anywhere and the driver said, "Let's go into the mess hall and have some coffee." There were four or five other buildings which were much smaller. One or two were repair workshops and a couple of them were for sleeping. We were in the mess hall having a cup of coffee when a guy walked in who was probably in his mid- 60s and he and the truck driver were old friends. I was introduced to him and his name was Bill Bower. I remarked how quiet it was there and he said that everyone was out in the field. The field was about a mile or so from camp and they came and went by truck, but he remained around camp all the time since he was the bull cook.

I said to him, "You're what?" He replied once again that he was the bull cook. My next question was "What's that?" and he answered, "You are obviously a stranger. I don't cook anything but I keep coal in the stove and take care of the dishes and sweep up around the mess hall and the stairway and the little things that the cook doesn't do. When I get my work done, I can do what I like and I enjoy it and have fun with the guys." The driver then had to leave as he had to go back to Fairbanks, but he wished me luck before he left.

I didn't have to wait long until the crews started to arrive for lunch. Bill introduced me to the foreman, Carl Brenner, and said after you have had your lunch, you will get on the truck with me. As the mess hall filled, I had never heard so many different accents in such a small area -- mostly from the mid-west, the western states and the south and a lot of Russians. Later I realized that I was the only Irish guy in the whole place.

When lunch was over I got on the truck and what a ride that was. You got up on the truck by grabbing hold of a big rope that had a large knot on the end of it and you swung up into the back end. The truck had two sides and a roof and a bench on each side. You held onto anything you could grab. It was a fun, wild ride. The guys jumped off at whatever camp they were working at.

I didn't know where I was working and stayed on and eventually I was the only one left. Eventually the truck came to a stop and Carl the foreman said, "Come with me." I looked around and there was nobody in sight anywhere – I was in "No Man's Land." It sure was a long way from New York City.

He said, "OK, this is what I want you to do. Do you see the markings here on the ground – I want you to dig a hole approximately six feet long and about three feet wide and I want it four feet deep. There is a pick and shovel over there." He asked me if I thought I could do that and I said, "Sure, I don't see any reason why I can't." He told me he was leaving but would be back later to pick me up. Before he left I asked him what the hole was for and he said, "That's to bury a dead man." He again told me he would be back later to pick me up. I looked at the departing truck and wondered to myself, why would anyone want to bury someone in this ice?

There wasn't a person anywhere and I couldn't even see the camp. I realized that that wasn't my problem. I had a hole to dig so I picked up the shovel and started to clear off the moss and debris from the marked area. Then I got the pick to loosen the surface soil and when the point of the pick hit the soil, it didn't even leave a mark. I hit it again and again and nothing. I might as well be hitting a granite wall. This was my introduction to permafrost.

The ground was frozen solid all the way down to bedrock, to whatever depth that would be since the beginning of time. I pounded and pounded and chopped and progress was next to impossible. I kept at it and at it and did I ever work. I kept thinking that if he wants to bury some guy four feet down, he is going to be very annoyed when he gets back to pick me up and sees how little I got done. This is going to be very interesting.

Later on the truck returned and Carl comes up and took a look at what I did and said, "What are you trying to do, kill yourself?" Apparently the little that I got done, which was practically nothing, was much more than I should have accomplished. To this day I still wonder if that was an initiation test.

I never was put on that detail again but that was my initiation to the gold fields. We went back on the truck to camp and I had my first dinner, which was delicious. I was told to go upstairs and wherever you find a room with an empty cot it's yours. The room only had a metal cot in it with a mattress which you put your sleeping bag on and there was a small shelf for your personal possessions.

Up the stairs to the left was a washroom which was about 8 or 9 feet wide and maybe 20 feet long. On the length of the wall was the wash area and there was a trough the whole length of it, which had a tin galvanized liner inside and against the wall about every three feet was a hot and cold faucet where six or seven people could wash up at the same time. They had a separate building for toilets and showers.

I located a cot to put my sleeping bag on -- no sheet or pillow and I didn't realize at that time that I wouldn't see any of those items for many years. After staking my claim to my sleeping quarters, I went outside where a group of guys were standing around talking. They didn't have anything else to do. I asked one of them if somebody had died in camp and he said, "No, why do you ask?"

I told them I had been digging a grave for someone and Carl Brenner said it was for a dead man. He started to laugh and I didn't think it was funny when someone dies. He said, "You don't know what a dead man is?" I thought it was when his heart stops and he stops breathing. He said, "Hell no, that's not what it is. It isn't a grave you were digging. Have you ever walked down a sidewalk and walked smack into a cable coming from a pole on an angle to the ground? Well that cable has to be attached to something in the ground and it's attached to a dead man which is usually a large chunk of wood about 2 feet by 5 feet, buried in the soil to support it. So there is no wake and no funeral." Wow, the things you learn.

The next morning at breakfast the guy sitting next to me asked me to pass the flapjacks. I had no idea what he wanted and he asked me again. I looked at him with my mouth open and he said, "How about hot cakes?" I said, "Oh sure, here you are." I figured I was going to have to learn a whole new language.

I really should describe what kind of an operation a gold field is. In Alaska most of the mining was placer mining, done from above ground. After the field was discovered, the first thing the company would do was try to determine the approximate size of the field and locate the mother lode – meaning what area contained the greatest concentration of the ore. This would be done by taking core samples and they would expand out from there and of course the farther away from the core you got, the ore got less and less and at a certain point the concentration wasn't dense enough to warrant the cost of removal.

After the field was surveyed and mapped, they knew exactly how deep you had to go to reach bedrock and it took years of work before any gold was removed. The major problem was the fact that the region was frozen solid all the way down to bedrock, so the most important requirement was they had to have access to huge amounts of water. This would be needed first to thaw the permafrost. This takes years to accomplish and once the water problem was resolved, the water had to be piped to the field to begin the process.

The source of this water came from about 70 miles away. The pipe carrying the water was approximately 4 feet in diameter and when it got to the field it would be at the top of a very high hill and when that came down the steep drop, the weight of the water created a pressure of approximately 200 pounds per square inch. This is how the stripping and thawing of the soil was done. The water was fed into a hydraulic water gun with a 4 inch nozzle. This water pressure was applied to the frozen soil 24 hours a day, 7 days a week and gradually melted away the frozen soil. I have no idea where the water ended up, probably in the ocean via the Yukon River. They had 5 or 6 of these hydraulic guns operating all the time. With the soil removed, they eventually got down to gravel and rocks, which were also frozen.

They could not wash away gravel and rocks so this had to be thawed by driving points, which were pipes that are approximately three-quarters-of-an-inch in diameter. Each has a point at the end of it with a hole for the water to get through and was approximately 10 feet long. This was inserted into a machine and water was pumped into the pipe and at the same time a heavy weight pounded it through the permafrost and another length was added to the point and this continued until you reached bedrock, which could be anywhere from10 feet to an excess of 100 feet. Points were driven every 15 feet and the machine was then removed and the pipes were connected to a permanent water supply under high water pressure, which forced the water down to bedrock and slowly started melting the ice on its way up. This took years of time before they could start the process of removing any gold.

Next, an artificial lake was excavated and filled with water to a depth of approximately 20 feet. The base of the gold dredge would then be assembled in the water and when that was afloat, the huge machinery, needed for its operation, would be assembled on deck. Piece by piece it would all be enclosed and this gold dredge would be capable of digging to a depth of 70 feet below water level.

The dredge operated 24-hours-a-day, 7 days a week and every 2 weeks the gold would be removed on what was called "Clean-up Day." The gold was scooped up and placed in steel boxes and the mercury and gold were handled the same way. Then it was transported to headquarters in Fairbanks by truck, with a driver and an armed guard. I believe the gold was separated from the mercury by evaporating the mercury through a heat process. This was raw gold – it went through a refining process and then it was poured into bricks and shipped to Fort Knox.

On my first day on the job I was on the bull gang. The next day after breakfast, the foreman told me I was going to the stripping operation, operating the hydraulic guns and I was warned that a few guys were killed on those so I shouldn't get careless.

Those crews, like the dredge crew, worked three shifts around the clock – usually three guys on each shift. It was very interesting because this is where the pre-historic animals had been found. We had to be very careful when one would start to appear and we would try to melt the permafrost around it without damaging the animal.

The University of Alaska had a division that would send reps out to the field where we were working to check on the progress of whatever animal was emerging in the hope that it would be in one piece. One Mammoth that was on display in the Museum of Natural History in New York City came out of Fairbanks Creek. I have about a foot long piece of ivory that came from the tusk of a mammoth.

The camp superintendent, Carl Johnson, was a very reserved man and a very decent, likeable person and a man of few words. When I went on the night shift, which we called the graveyard shift, you were there all alone all night and of course it was daylight all the time and you didn't speak a word to another human being.

Early in the morning, Carl would come by and following him would be his cocker spaniel, named Penny, walking three paces behind him – never more and never less. I would smile to myself because they always reminded me of Queen Elizabeth and Prince Phillip. They would never come closer than about a hundred yards and he would give a hand wave that reminded me of Miss America. Every day the same routine and I often wondered if he knew my name. But he treated everyone the same and everybody thought very highly of him.

I found the graveyard shift very difficult. You rotated every two weeks and just when you were getting used to it, it was time to change. The day crew's breakfast was at seven thirty every morning and after breakfast they went out to the fields. As they got dropped off, we got picked up so we had breakfast at eight thirty. If I ate breakfast, I could never fall asleep, so I wouldn't eat breakfast, and I always told the guys that if I was asleep at noon, don't wake me up for lunch. Most times I slept through lunch and therefore missed breakfast and lunch. I would always be up by five thirty in the evening, which was dinner time but at that point I wanted bacon and eggs, not meat and vegetables. I didn't have to worry about gaining weight.

Camp life was very good – there were always people to talk with. We had a lot of fun. I completely forgot that I should have reported for work in San Diego a month ago. The date came and went and I had forgotten that Safeway ever existed.

At Gold Stream camp, Bill Bower, the bull cook, and I became very good friends and we would go target shooting in the evenings. One day he got talking about his farm and when he reached the age of 60, he and his wife decided to sell their farm in Iowa and they bought a camper to travel around the United States. He told me they got as far as California and were camping at a campsite and he got up one morning and went for a walk and he never returned. He deliberately kept going until he finally arrived in Fairbanks. He never made contact with his wife or two sons again. There was no way to trace him because in those days, farmers didn't pay Social Security so he never had a Social Security number. He told me he had no intention of ever contacting them. He never gave me a reason why he did this and it was over seven years since he left, so he figured at this time he would legally be declared dead and that was the way he wanted it.

Around the end of Sept. the weather put a stop to all mining. The camps were closed down and would remain closed until mid-March. Every year on St. Patrick's Day you would return to one of the camps. For many of the workers, this was their life. This was their family. If they had a family anywhere, nobody ever heard them speak of them and you didn't ask. When you met someone, you usually asked them where they were from and they would tell you and that was the end of the questions. Sometimes I really thought that everyone around me was an orphan.

When camp closed, they would return to Fairbanks, check into the Nordale Hotel where they had booked their room for the winter months and in the spring return to the gold fields. They had done this their whole life. We would meet on the street and stop and talk. Usually they would be nicely dressed; might be walking around smoking a cigar and be as happy as can be. Alaskans are certainly a breed unto themselves.

I had met a guy in camp whose name was Johnny Yogas from Long Island. We became good friends. When the camp closed, Johnny asked me what I was going to do for the winter. He was wondering if I was returning to New York. My immediate response was, "Heck, No." I asked him if he was going back, and he said, "No way – are you kidding?" We rented a cabin that had two cots and a stove. It was in a tiny little village that had four houses total and a trading post with a post office. It was called, Fox, Alaska, and it was less than a block from the mess hall in Gold Stream camp.

It had a wood stove so we were as snug as a bug in a rug in the horrendous winter. We spent most of our time in Fairbanks and Johnny spent most of that time in the many bars that were there. He liked to drink and I had never had a drink in my life. Johnny owned a car which gave us great access to Fairbanks.

My not drinking became quite a problem. Everyone would insist that I have a drink so it got to the point where I hardly ever went into a bar. If I did, someone would always say, "You have to have a drink" and no matter what I said, it didn't matter. They kept insisting. Bartenders that knew me would come to my defense and would tell them to get off my case and leave me alone. This was a constant battle so eventually I refused to go into the bars. They were wild and out of control. A glass of beer in the states at that time cost 15 cents. There you would get a can of beer with two holes punched in it and it cost 50 cents. There were no pull off tabs on cans back then.

CHAPTER 7

During the Iron Curtain period, the U.S. believed the Russian invasion would take place across the Bering Strait into Alaska, and then head south to the mainland U.S. At this time the DEW Line was put in operation. This was a line that went across the tip of Alaska and Canada. Dew Line is short for Distant Early Warning. From this, the U.S. would get their first warning if they were being invaded. Some miles inland they put the second warning stations which were called the White Alice Line. Fairbanks had two huge Air Bases – Eielson Air Force Base was 26 miles south of Fairbanks and Ladd Air Force Base was six miles south of Fairbanks. They also had thousands of Army personnel stationed there for arctic training in case they ended up fighting the Russians from Siberia.

The U.S jets patrolled the International Date Line twenty four hours a day during the summer months. There are two islands in the Bearing Straight – Big Diamede and Little Diamede, and they are three miles apart. Big Diamede is in Russia and Little Diamede is in the U.S. The natives are all intermarried so they would go back and forth to visit their families. When the Iron Curtain closed they still went to visit but that stopped when the ones who went previously were imprisoned and never returned.

The next thing I knew, it was St. Patrick's Day and back to reality. March 17th was the day when we returned to Gold Stream Camp. There was ice and snow everywhere. I was wondering what we might be doing under those conditions. I didn't have long to wait as our job was to set up a boiler on the ground in front of Dredge 8 and get it in operation. The purpose of the boiler was to generate steam and the steam would be used to cut the ice so that we could get the dredge afloat.

The cutters were made of 3/4 " pipe in the shape of a rectangle, approximately 3' by 6' and at the bottom end there was a row of pin holes facing down. The top end had a connection which was to connect the flexible steam hose to. When the steam came up to the required pressure, you opened the valve and the steam shot out of the pinholes. This cut through the ice which was five feet thick; the depth to which the lake froze in that winter. When the three feet by three feet by five feet blocks were cut, a steel cable was put around them and they were lifted out by a crane and eventually the dredge was floating once again.

The welder was very busy making all sorts of repairs on the dredge and I was sent to help him. I knew nothing about welding but the welder was a very nice guy and explained a lot of things to me and taught me how to weld. I was doing pretty well and one morning the dredge master came over to me and said, "The welder is unable to work as his eyes were damaged by an electric flash and he was unable to see."

He hoped to be able to return in a few days and he found me a helper so that I could be the welder. I said, "Wait a minute, I am not a welder." His reply was, "You are now – I have seen you welding and you can do it. This job has to get done today." I said, "If you are ordering me to do it, that's fine with me but remember the first time you drop the bucket line and all the steel plates go sliding into the lake, don't come complaining to me." His answer was, "I know you can do it" and I did.

A short time later he asked me if I would like to stay on the dredge crew – he needed a stern oiler and I thought I'd like that. He agreed to have them transfer me over to that crew. Now I found myself on the extreme back end of the dredge, about fifty feet up in the air where the tailings exit and every two hours I would have to make a complete round and grease hundreds of fittings on the conveyor belt rollers and grease the motors and the gears. This was the area where the huge screen was where the water pressure was spraying.

After a few months, I noticed that every light I saw had a huge halo around it and it seemed to be getting worse. I was getting worried so I went to an eye specialist in Fairbanks and he examined my eyes and then he checked the pressure on them and said, "The pressure on your eyes is so high that your eyes actually could explode." He asked if I had any idea of what was causing it and he asked what kind of work I did. I told him about the very fine mist in the air from the high water pressure and there probably are minute particles of very fine sand in the air. His advice was, "You cannot remain in that environment – if you do you will lose your sight."

I explained to the company what was happening and they said, "No Problem". Carl Johnson, the guy that I didn't think even knew my name asked me if I knew how to operate a Hoist. I didn't know what it was and he told me that he would like to send me to Eldorado Camp and have me operate that equipment. He told me that it was in storage now but would be ready in a few days. He told me he would explain the operation of the equipment and was sure I would have no problem operating it in a few days.

So, once again, I was moving. I arrived in Eldorado Camp and moved into my new suite and rolled out my sleeping bag and unpacked my toiletries and was ready to go to work. I noticed there was no dredge so apparently they hadn't advanced in the thawing to that extent. That would come later. However, Carl took me out to introduce me to my new job. I was the only one there. They had put up a shack to protect the equipment and the controls and what I liked about it was that if it rained, I would be protected and it was a straight day shift. The purpose of all this was to keep the camp from being flooded out from all the water that was being used in the field. It was a very narrow channel that the excess water had to exit through and my job was to insure that this passage was to remain open.

Carl gave me very thorough instructions and I was shocked he could talk so much. It was all business and he spoke as if he was being charged a dollar a word but he was really very nice and told me if I had any problems with anything just to let him know. So here I was once again, at the most remote end of the mine field – all alone and I didn't even get back to camp for lunch. The cook packed a lunch for me but I really enjoyed the operation and I did have a friend who joined me for lunch every day; a little creature called a shrew. He's a little larger than a mouse but they claim he must eat three times his body weight each day in order to survive. He and I became great friends.

The crew at Eldorado was very enjoyable. There were the usual gatherings around the mess hall because there really wasn't anything else to do and everyone enjoyed each other's company and there never was a problem. I used to read a lot but never got bored. I remained in Eldorado for the rest of the season and decided that when the season was over I was going to go to Ireland to see mom and the rest of the family.

I flew from Fairbanks to Seattle/Tacoma Airport and I then traveled by Greyhound Bus across the country to New York. I visited my friends; the Campions for a week and sailed out of New York to Ireland on the MV Britannic III. I was five-and-a-half days at sea and landed in Cobh in County Cork and expected to catch a train to Roscommon, in the west of Ireland and was told there was only one train leaving for there each day.

I came through customs and saw a fast-talking little guy with his cap down over one eye who was working there. I asked him if he could help me and told him I needed to get to the train station so I could get to the west of Ireland. He told me he would get me there on time and he said "God Bless You" so many times and how good it was to have met me that I should have been suspicious. He assured me I didn't have to worry about a thing so I gave him a big tip and found out that the train had left the station much earlier and the next one was tomorrow.

Welcome to Ireland, Malachy. I should have known better. I had to spend the night in Cove and called my mom and told her I would be home tomorrow. She didn't know I was coming to Ireland and was very surprised. It was wonderful to see all the family. My little brothers and sisters weren't so little anymore – in fact the youngest, Anita, was a teenager but they really were strangers to me and I was a stranger to them.

My older sisters and brothers didn't change much and mom didn't change at all – she looked great. The village was pretty much the same and most of the people were still there. Overall they were living much better than when I left four years before. The standard of living had improved immensely. The forge in the yard was still there. Joe and George were still shaping the hot iron and the neighbors still came in to shoot the breeze. My friends were still there – it was strange that everything seemed the same but nothing was. I thought they just weren't like they used to be – they had changed. Even my best friend wasn't the same – there was something strange about everyone. Then I began to wonder if maybe it was me that changed, that maybe that old saying is true, "You can never go back."

Kevin, Eamon and I took a trip to England and stayed there for about a week. We had a really nice time and when we got back I did some work around the house. I was there for Christmas and it was the first time in years that mom had all her children together for this holiday. This made her very happy. I stayed there for about three months and bought a car to use while I was there and left it to them when I left. I visited the farm where I had spent so much of my life and it was very different now, all livestock and no tillage. I drove around a small area but really wasn't that interested in traveling – I didn't visit many relatives; I was just content to stay around home.

For my return to the U.S., I had purchased a ticket on the S.S. Olympia that was built in Scotland and was on its maiden voyage. It picked up its first passengers in Scotland and its next stop was Dublin, Ireland and that's where I boarded. From there it sailed to Southampton in England and then went to Cherbourg in France and back to Cobh in the south of Ireland. Here I was back in Ireland, a few days after I had left. It finally headed across the Atlantic and five or six days later we arrived in Halifax, Nova Scotia and then to New York City. We were at sea for a total of eleven days.

This was not an ordinary sailing. First of all there was a labor strike the day the ship sailed so they left with a skeleton crew. As a result, the meals were very slow getting to the dining area and when they arrived they were ice cold. When a ship is on its maiden voyage, at each port of entry the water canons are fired and escort the ship into port. The Lord-Mayor of that city comes aboard with a group of entertainers that put on a show for the passengers and crew.   Following the show there was a dinner party and in front of each place setting was a bottle of Heineken beer.

I shared a cabin with an Australian. He originally came from northern Ireland. When he immigrated to Australia they were looking for people to immigrate. They paid your expense of travel and after five years you would refund the cost to the government.

When the period ended, the government sent him a letter reminding him that the money was due and he ignored it. A second letter was sent which he also ignored. A third and final letter reminded him of the consequences if he didn't meet his obligations. They would refuse to issue him a passport to leave the country. He wrote them a letter and told them he would send them a postcard from Piccadilly. He told me he did keep his word and mailed them a post card. What they didn't know was that he had a seaman's passport and that was how he got out of Australia.

At the special ship's dinner, many people didn't drink beer so the bottles remained untouched, but the caps had been removed. When everyone left the dining room, this guy went from table to table and picked up as many bottles as he could and carried them to our cabin and stood them on the deck. He made several trips up and down before the dining room was empty. He could drink beer like no one I had ever seen.

We had bunk beds in the cabin and I slept on the top bunk, thank God. That night while we were asleep the ocean got rough and I woke up and I thought someone was hitting the bulkhead with a hammer. I put the light on to see what was happening and the bottles were lying on their sides. The ladder had fallen down and was riding on top of the bottles which were empty at this point.

When the ship rolled to starboard side, the bottles would roll and the ladder would be on top of them and would hit the bulkhead with a bang and then when the ship rolled to the port side, the action reversed. The next morning the cabin smelled like a brewery and the rug was soaking with beer. The ship sent a staff in with vacuum cleaners and steamers and days later when we landed in New York, the ship still stunk like a brewery. I often wondered if they ever got the odor out of that cabin.

I was looking forward to returning to Alaska. When I returned to New York, I contacted Johnny Yogas and we planned a date when we would leave New York for our trip back to Alaska. This time we were going to drive back to Fairbanks.

CHAPTER 8

I stayed in New York for about a week and went to visit my old friends on 140th Street and Willis Avenue. I went to a dance at the Jaeger House and I asked a girl to dance. We were talking and she asked me where I was living and I told her I was just passing through. She wanted to know where I was going and when I told her Alaska, she told me she had an uncle that lived there. I asked her where in Alaska and she told me he lived in Fairbanks. She told me his name and I was shocked because I had read in the paper just before I left there about this guy that was out on the trail and apparently had gotten very sick and he knew he was going to die and didn't want the wolves to find his body. They believe he lay down in a glacier and froze himself in the ice. I remembered the name because it was a real Irish name and it was the same name she mentioned. I was shocked but I kept my mouth shut because I didn't want to upset her.

As we had planned, Johnny picked me up in the Bronx and we went through the Holland Tunnel into New Jersey. Johnny was driving and he crossed a double yellow line and when we exited the tunnel the police were waiting for us and issued him a ticket. I guess that was our going away present from the State of New York. Sometime later we entered the state of Ohio and were in the little town of Wooster when the car broke down. We were towed to a repair shop and after an extensive examination of the car they told us what the problem was and that they would have to order the part. They didn't say where the part was coming from but we figured it must have come from Ethiopia because they needed at least three days before they could install it and we could leave town. The car did get repaired and it did take three days and it was the most boring town to get stuck in – it was the pits. There was nothing there.

They had one movie theatre, the only show started at seven thirty and it was the same movie every night for a week. Johnny couldn't believe that he would get stuck in a "dry town". All they were allowed to serve by law was 3.2 beer which was like drinking water for Johnny and they served wine but nothing else. Johnny wasn't a happy camper so for three days we hung around the bar and listened to the farmers telling us about the state of Ohio. There just wasn't anything in the entire country to equal it as far as they were concerned. The bartender became our best friend. He said it was so good to talk to people other than farmers who were winos. He was sorry when we were leaving. I know we weren't sorry to be leaving.

We were on our way again and stopped off to visit the battleground of the Little Big Horn in Montana, which is where Custer's Last Stand took place. We also stopped at the Petrified Forest in South Dakota. We arrived at the Canadian border crossing in Sweet Grass, Montana where the Customs Inspector asked if we had anything to declare and we said "No". He asked if we had any booze or alcohol and Johnny told them he had a case of beer.

The inspector wanted to know how many cans were in a case and Johnny told him there were 24 cans in a case and he said, "Now you have exactly 22 cans too many." Johnny asked him what we were supposed to do with it now. The inspector told him that you can drink it if you want but you are not taking it into Canada. While you are in Canada, Her Majesty's Beer will have to be good enough for you. Johnny's answer was "F- - - Your Majesty and her Beer" and turns around and walks out of the Custom's House and I follow him. At this point, I am saying to myself, "Thank God we are on American soil – and luckily we are not on the other side of the border with an answer like that."

We got into the car and drove into the little town of Sweet Grass and found a bar and Johnny picks up the case of beer and hands it to the bartender and says, "Have a drink on us." Back we went to the border and I was praying that we didn't meet the same inspector and luckily we didn't. Now we were in the Province of Alberta, which is flat, prairie land. About an hour later we could see in the distance an intersection and there were two people standing on the roadside.

There was nobody – not another car in sight and as we got closer we could see that they were in uniform. We figured we were in trouble now. The inspector probably phoned ahead and they were standing there waiting for us. They put their hands up for us to stop. They pulled us over and one of them walked over to the car, opened the gas tank cover and pushed a plastic tube into the tank. He pulled it out and looked at it and closed the tank and said it was OK for us to go. We asked him what that was all about. He said, "The ranches around here are subsidized by the government for the fuel they use at the ranch but they cannot use that fuel in their cars." They could tell if it was the subsidized fuel because it was of a different color. That is what they were checking and when we left them we gave a big sigh of relief.

Alberta was a nice province, rolling hills, a lot of oil wells and farm land everywhere. As you traveled northwest it began to change and got a lot more rugged. Days passed and we entered the Alcan Highway, which was the name at that time. This later was changed to the Alaskan Highway. This highway is approximately 1,500 miles long. We slept high in the Canadian Rockies in the car and the next day was Easter Sunday. It was not a good time to be traveling in Canada as they take Easter very seriously. Road houses were very sparse and we depended on them for gas and oil. Back then you could get gas and oil but that was all you could get on Easter Sunday.

We drove 800 miles to get breakfast and arrived on Easter Monday in Whitehorse only to be told that Easter Monday is also a holiday. I said to Johnny, "If Easter doesn't end soon you and I are going to starve." Johnny had that covered too.

That's when Johnny opened the car trunk and opened up this big, long hard salami. It was so hard you would need an ax to cut it, but Johnny had an answer for that, he came up with a monstrous hunting knife that could cut the salami. That was our sumptuous Easter celebration and of course, Johnny was thinking if it wasn't for that Customs Inspector, he would have had a much better Easter dinner.

By now we were in the Yukon Territory and the weather there changed very rapidly. It was very mountainous. When it rained high in the mountains, the water came down with such force, roads and bridges just disappeared. I had driven this highway five times and the last time I swore I would never drive it again. It was an absolute nightmare. I will never, ever forget it. It was like being in the middle of the Atlantic Ocean and it could change just as rapidly. No matter when I traveled it or how often I saw it, this far-north country takes my breath away.

Only God could create something so rough, rugged, lonely and so unforgiving -- yet, it was so breathtakingly beautiful. Whether it was the Yukon, the Northwest Territories or Alaska, it was beyond description. We finally arrived at the Yukon, Alaska border and got through Customs easily. We crossed the border and lost two hours. Later, the highway twisted and turned around the mountains so many times that you found yourself back in the Yukon again. You came in and went out several times – it was not watch friendly territory.

It was still a long distance to Fairbanks but we finally arrived. The trip took us twelve days because we lost three days in Ohio for the car to be repaired. It was great to be back. Johnny and I parted company because he was going back to Gold Stream Camp and I was going to Eldorado. When I sat down to lunch, my faithful little friend, the shrew, arrived like I had never left. I was so glad to see he survived the winter. The weather was terrible; it was the wettest summer I had ever seen. The clouds rolled over the hilltops, dropped into the valley and we never saw the hilltops all summer. I was happy to have my little shack where it was nice and dry. Nothing exciting happened – it was the regular routine but everyone was happy to see the season end.

I returned to Fairbanks and got myself a place to stay for the winter. It was a rooming house run by a couple from Wisconsin. She was a wonderful cook and was like a mother to us. Two other guys stayed there also. Her husband, whose name was Hank, was a carpenter who had been injured and was unable to work. I didn't want to spend another winter doing nothing so I got a job in the Northern Commercial Company in the grocery division.

It was an unusual operation. They sold clothing, sporting equipment, guns and ammunition, fishing equipment, cameras and food all on one floor. A large part of their business was catering to prospectors. You only saw them when they came in to pay their bills and they left a listing of their needs for the next year or longer. They would leave instructions and dates where they would be. Their supplies would be dropped by a Bush Pilot.

I enjoyed living at 303 Minnie Street and Maureen Campion wrote to me and kept me up to date about what was happening in the Bronx. She was very good about writing.

March finally arrived and I returned to Eldorado. One morning Carl came to visit me in my shack. That was his first visit since I returned and he asked me to shut the equipment down as he wanted to talk to me. He started by saying that he had a question to ask me, but first he wanted to explain the situation before I gave him an answer.

The company owned a gold field in an area called Hogatza on the Hog River. In 1939 they sent a crew there to start the development process and they erected a few cabins but World War II broke out and they stopped the project. There was very little information known about the project. There wasn't anyone in the company that was familiar with the operation and only very crude maps of the area existed.

Headquarters put Carl in charge of this operation and they had pinpointed a location on the Koyukuk River that they believed was somewhere near the location of the gold field. Their plan was to have a river barge deliver the necessary equipment to this site to establish a base camp. From that location we would have to locate the gold field and make it accessible by building a road. The total crew could not exceed five, including himself. He would have to assemble two Butler Huts that would be transported on the river barge.

One of the huts would go to the cook and that would have to double as a dining room and his sleeping quarters and the other cabin would sleep the other four. Carl could pick from any camp in the area as to who he wanted to take with him.

He then told me he would like if I would go with him but he said, "Before you answer me I want you to know that if you refuse, there will be no hard feelings. This certainly is a trip into the unknown with total isolation deep into the interior. I don't know what to expect and neither does anyone else. Think it over for a few days and let me know when you reach a decision."

I said to him, "Ok, I thought about it and I will go with you." He replied, "That's great. You will report to headquarters next week and start assembling the two cabins." I was to continue living in camp and would be picked up in the morning and returned to camp every evening. A few days later I had to say good bye to my little shrew and I actually felt bad leaving him but it was time to go.

Now, I was moving once again but this time it appeared that we would be moving to another planet. A few days later, I arrived at headquarters and met the two other guys, Ernie Botts and Ralph Harlan. They were nice guys; Ernie came from Minnesota and Ralph came from Seattle, Washington.

The guys in camp really gave me a hard time. "Hey, Donoghue, I hear you are going to the ass end of nowhere – why not go a little west and cross over to Siberia – at least you would have someone to talk to?" The next question was, "Why were you asked and why did you agree to go?" My answer was "How the hell do I know? I was asked and I said OK and that's all there is to it."

We spent the next couple of weeks putting the cabins together. The major problem was securing insulation to the steel beams. We had to drill so many holes into the beams and attach wood strips so we could attach the plywood outside the insulation which was 12" thick on the walls and the ceiling. This would be our only protection, if we were to survive in sub-zero temperatures.

When we completed all the things that were required, it was loaded on a barge on the Chena River and started the journey. When they estimated the arrival time, we were picked up by the Bush Pilot and flown to Hogatza. We could see the barge from the air; it had arrived and was tied up on the river bank. A pontoon landing is quite a thrill. We climbed down from the plane onto the pontoon. The pilot brought the plane as close as he could to the barge. We then waded through the water and climbed onto the barge. The water temperature was about a half degree above freezing. We stood and looked at the shore, it was a jungle.

Luckily the barge had a steel ramp that could reach the bank. Wet and cold from our wading through the water, we immediately had to get to work. We had to get ashore so we cranked up the D8 caterpillar and plowed our way through the underbrush. Time was critical; we had to quickly clear an area to unload the barge, so it could start on its return journey to pick up the next load.

Carl said that when we finished unloading the barge, we would enlarge the storage area to make room for future deliveries. This would be our permanent base camp. After that we worked on assembling the large crane that would unload the heavy machinery when it arrived.

When an area was cleared, the first thing to be taken care of was our new homes. We unloaded our two homes and when we built them, we put them on runners and attached a steel cable so that anytime we had to move camp, we would just connect the cable to a bulldozer and off we could go to another location. We set them in a corner of the clearing and they looked like doll houses. Only then did it hit me that this was all that was between us and the elements. I wondered how it would feel when the temperature in the winter reached fifty or sixty below zero, or colder in this region.

The next question was where to store the drums of gasoline and diesel. This was not something you wanted to have near where you sleep or work. What a fireball that would be.

The next morning it started all over again. If only we could get this barge out of here, maybe we could get some rest. It took several days to unload and then finally we could relax and have time to survey our surroundings.

When the barge and its crew left the dock and started its turn to go south on the river, they were waving at us. We looked at each other and someone said, "That's our last connection with the rest of the world, but we do have a short-wave radio somewhere in this mess." That was if we ever found it and got it set up, we would be able to make contact with headquarters in Fairbanks, at least that was what they told us.

The company had made contact with the natives of an Indian village about seventy miles down on the Yukon River in a village called Huslia and promised to hire anyone that wanted to work. They were delighted for the opportunity and about eight of them moved their wives, children and sled dogs up river and set up a tent village and a temporary trading post not far from our camp on the opposite side of the Koyukuk River. They worked with Ralph at the base camp unloading equipment and assembling the mess hall. The mess hall was too large to be shipped assembled.

The owner of the barge was the son of a French father and an Indian mother from the Athapaskan Tribe. His wife was also Athapaskan Indian. This was the company connection to the Indians. They really were very pleasant people.

They told us they never had a job before, as they were hunters. Carl laughed when he looked at the job applications -- when it came to the questions of color of eyes and color of hair, everyone had the same. Later when the camp would expand, the men would move to our camp.

The wife of the barge owner ran the trading post. She was a delightful woman who told me she had never gone to school, but she taught herself how to read by studying the labels on the cans and boxes in the store.

Two more huts had to be assembled, one to house the motors and controls as we had to protect them from the weather. We had to install the motors and controls and the diesel engines and connect all the cables to the drums. After all that, we hoped it would work. The second building was a bunkhouse for the operator of the stiff leg. He had to be there at all times loading and unloading so we didn't know if the second structure could wait until more manpower came. Sure enough, Carl wanted this thing to be operational before we did anything else. This structure didn't need to be insulated so it wasn't a big job. We installed everything and were surprised that everything worked and were glad to be finished with it.

All of our supplies had to remain at the landing site. We then set up a large tent and activated a generator to keep our perishables refrigerated. This system remained in use through the next year.

Carl got his compasses activated and pointed it in the direction the road would go. Now our job was to build a road from the landing site to the gold field, wherever that was. This road was going to be built with the two D8's – number fifty five and number seventy three. My buddy had number fifty five and I was assigned number seventy three. Carl would leave the markers for us to follow. We weren't given a timetable but we knew the company figured we would be at our destination in approximately two months. When we would finish about three or four miles of road, we would move the camp forward. We continued to fight our way into the tundra. Trees, brush and anything else would be piled up almost to the roofs of the two shacks.

One night I woke up and had to go to the bathroom. Half asleep, I got up and stumbled outside and took care of business and just then I looked up and standing on the top of the debris and staring down on the top of my head was this huge black bear. Of course it was broad daylight, as if it were the middle of the afternoon. We could have shook hands with each other. That's what you get when there is no bathroom available. I would have been happier to see my little shrew friend. I slowly walked back to camp and the bear ignored me.

We finally got the radio set up and it required an aerial of about one hundred feet and it had to be installed at a great height to be effective. That would be no problem if we were located in the California Redwoods. Our campsite was chosen by the height of the trees. All we needed was just one tree. When we were located in a mountainous region, we wouldn't get any reception at all. At times we could pick up a station in New Delhi, India, loud and clear and nothing else. Other times we could pick up taxi drivers in Honolulu speaking to each other in their cabs but we couldn't reach nearby Fairbanks. It all depended on the openings between the mountains where we were located. At one time, we had a three week period with absolutely no communication or mail delivery due to weather. We joked about it, and used to say that World War III could have started and ended and we wouldn't even know it was going on.

The squaws spent all summer fishing. They would catch salmon in their nets and I would sit and watch them when they were pulling in their nets. Large salmon would be tangled in the net and they would hit them between the eyes with a large club. That took the fight out of them. Then they would throw them in the boat and when they came ashore they would clean and gut them and split them lengthways from head to tail but would leave both halves connected at the tail so they could hang the fish on a pole above a wood fire and dry and smoke it. This was their food supply for the sled dogs for the winter.

I went to visit the natives in their camp many times. I would sit on the riverbank with the men and talk and would see that the women were working non-stop putting up poles, cutting firewood, cleaning salmon and the men would be sitting there smoking their pipes. I asked them how come they were not helping with some of the work and the answer I got was, "We don't do that – that's women's work. We are hunters." I don't think that would fly in our society.

One day we were having lunch and one of the natives pointed out another brother across the way. He told me, "See that man over there – he killed my father." I said to him, "What do you mean that he killed your father? How did he do that?" His answer was, "He shot him in the head." I asked him why he shot him and his answer was, "My father went crazy and we don't have any place to put crazy people so the elders of the village pulled straws and that man got the short straw and it was up to him to take care of him and put him out of his misery." He said it very nonchalantly; no big deal, it was part of a regular conversation.

Owning money didn't have much meaning to them. I remember sitting watching them playing poker after they received their monthly pay. They were paid in cash each month because they would have no way of cashing their checks while our pay remained in a vault at headquarters until we got back. We wouldn't have been able to cash it if they did send it and we had nothing to spend it on anyhow.

There were five or six natives sitting around a table playing poker and I watched one of them lose a month's pay in less than an hour. While he was playing poker, he was also strumming on a banjo and all that time he never missed a beat on the banjo. Even when everything was gone, he continued playing the banjo and wasn't the least bit phased by his loss. It had no meaning. They lived off the land and earned their money trading furs. That was sufficient for their existence.

Things were going rather smoothly on the job. Ralph and Ernie and the natives were busy at the landing site sorting things out and moving things into different areas. They also assembled and insulated the other buildings. They could drive from wherever our camp was located over the new road that we had completed.

We had finished about eight miles of the road when we were stopped dead in our tracks. Carl had run into an area of swamp land that all it was capable of supporting was our body weight. It was three miles wide but was so large an area; we were unable to see where it ended.

We knew that the Koyukuk River was on our left and this was caused by the river so there was no point in going in that direction. When we looked to the right, there was no end in sight; all we could see was swamp. Carl called headquarters on the radio and made the report. They were shocked. This was the last thing on earth they expected to hear. All they said was, "We'll get back to you." A few hours later they told us they were sending a bush plane out tomorrow with one of the company executives on board and they would fly over the area to see if there was a way around it.

The plane arrived the next day but couldn't land anywhere. They flew all over the area and they got back to us and told us, "It is so vast; there is no way around it." This is a disaster. I was totally shocked at my own reaction. I felt like someone had kicked me in the stomach. I had no idea of how involved I had become in this operation. You would think it was my fault. Then I just got very annoyed at all the brains and all the engineering degrees that were floating around. Wouldn't you think that someone would have had the brains to have flown over the area and discovered the miles and miles of swamp before sending us here? They couldn't have missed it if they had. All I wondered was where it was going from here. I thought I was the only idiot but the other guys felt worse than me. As little as Carl spoke before, he spoke even less now.

The engineering department suggested that laying trees and branches on the surface of the swamp and covering them with gravel should make it navigational. This would have to be a priority in order to get it done before the winter got too severe. Things really got moving. This worked out well but the lost time ended all hopes of reaching our goal until sometime the following year.

The natives departed in early Aug. as they had to hunt for their meat supply for the coming winter and prepare their trap lines to get the skins, which was their financial support. This was their priority. They dismantled their tents and prepared their wives and children for the trip back to Huslia. They took along all their dried salmon, as this would be the food supply for their dogs all winter when the rivers were frozen and no fish was available. We would see them again next year.

Aug. 27th we had the first snowfall that stayed on the ground and it was still there the following June. We had some snow on and off before that but it didn't stay. The work kept going and the road got longer and longer and we finally reached the other side of the swamp. In the meantime, the barge arrived with another delivery, which would be the last one of the season.

Three more buildings arrived that had to be assembled. Ralph was busy on that job. The stiff leg worked perfectly and made the unloading much easier. Ernie, Carl and I went back to road building. By now winter had arrived and the company was getting disturbed. After all this time, we had not found the gold fields, in fact we didn't even know where they were.

We kept building the road and Carl kept marking the way. He wondered if the compass was defective. We didn't know. The days were getting shorter and shorter rapidly. By now we were into Oct. and road-building was finished for the winter. The most we could do at this point was blast a trail by getting rid of the brush and tundra and we were able to freight over the frozen ground. Daylight had practically disappeared. The snow started to pile up and the temperature was getting colder. We moved one of the sheds up to our camp and we moved the gas and diesel fuel near where we camped. We had cleared an area large enough for a landing strip so when we returned next spring, we would be able to land on skis. Carl told us we were going to have a visitor coming to see us.

"The CEO of United States Smelting, Refining and Mining Company will be here tomorrow." We asked Carl. "What the hell is he coming here for?" Carl's answer was, "He probably wants to see what we have been doing." We said, "That's good, maybe he can tell us where we are and better still, tell us where we are going." It is strange when you live in an environment under those conditions it does have an effect on your brain, your whole thinking process changes. You seem to be much more aware of the environment you are living in – wet, dry, hot, cold, daylight, darkness, work and sleep. There was no room for anything else. There was nothing to distract us and this became so much a part of you, and the rest of the world, as far as you were concerned, didn't seem to exist.

This seemed to affect you one of two ways. I had seen guys come here and within one week, they became basket cases. They actually had to fly a plane in and get them out as they couldn't deal with it. The other group had no affect, whatsoever. I actually enjoyed it. The U.S. Government actually developed a test that they would give guys that they were sending out to the DEW Line and the White Alice Line to see if they were capable of living in that environment. Well, according to the test – the Eskimos could not live and could not survive in that environment – so much for tests.

The next day the CEO arrived, accompanied by his Master Mechanic. It wasn't at all what I had expected; he was a very normal guy with no airs about him. He asked Carl if he could arrange for a trip so that we could see if we could locate the gold field. Carl said we could do that, but you must understand that the only way this can be done is with a bulldozer. You could not attempt to travel otherwise. Carl said he would set up an Athy Wagon behind the dozer and he and his friend could ride on that. This was a wagon that has no wheels, it rides on tracks. Carl told me that I was going to be the driver. He asked me to service the tractor as we would be leaving camp at four in the morning. That didn't matter much as there was practically no daylight at that time of year.

At this point, we had a couple of feet of snow on the ground and the temperature was in the forty degree below zero region. I don't know what they told the cook to pack for food, I think they may have given him the impression that we would be home for lunch. At four a.m. I cranked up the dozer and the CEO, Bill, and the mechanic, Jack, got up on the wagon. Carl got up on the dozer with me and he had a big flashlight and some maps and of course, his trusty compass. We left camp in frigid weather. In a few minutes we ran out of road and we turned into "No man's land."

Carl pointed the way as he was trying to read the map and the compass with a flashlight. When the blade of the dozer would hit a tree, snow would come showering down and within a few minutes of leaving the camp, we were ankle deep in snow. We were traveling blind. The lights on the dozer were iced up and you couldn't see ten feet ahead. Then another small tree would get knocked over and another shower of snow, mixed with ice, would land on your lap. We had a roof over us but all sides were open.

Daylight came for a short time but we knew that it would be gone again in a couple of hours. The danger of traveling in the woods was if you hit a tree in those temperatures, the tree was frozen and it would snap in the middle and it could possibly come down and hit the middle of the roof and kill us. You couldn't see this in time to slow down and come to a stop and ease the blade slowly against the tree in order to push it over slowly. By three in the afternoon, we were traveling along the top of a ridge looking down on a deep valley and Bill asked me to stop. He wanted me to go down into the valley and travel up the valley floor. Carl didn't agree with him and said we are on much safer ground up here and we have no idea what the conditions were down there, but the boss insisted, so I had to bring the dozer down to where he wanted it.

I knew Carl didn't want any part of this as we had been traveling almost eleven hours at this time, with no break. We were cold, numb, tired and hungry and suddenly the ground disappeared from under us and we were slowly sinking into a glacier. We jumped out and watched the dozer and the wagon slowly sink into the ground. We felt as though our hearts sunk with it.

We grabbed a few things off the wagon before it went down further. Someone grabbed two pairs of snowshoes and someone else grabbed the bag and that was all that was saved. There was no way to describe this situation. I think at that time there was no question in anyone's mind that our chances of survival were nil. Later we were told that the temperature that day was fifty three degrees below zero. We stood there and still there was no sign of the cabins. They were the only objects that would tell us that we had arrived at the gold field. We figured the cabins had to be closer to us than our camp. We had left eleven hours earlier. We had to decide which direction we should go.

Someone glanced into the bag and said they thought there was food in it but we had enough problems to worry about other than that right now. We figured we would head for the cabins and didn't think they could be that far away. We only had two pairs of snow shoes and four people and the question was, "Who is good at using snow shoes?" I certainly wasn't but Carl said he was good on them but Jack, the master mechanic, told us he had never worn a pair. So that left the CEO, Bill, who said he had used them before. They would lead the trail and we would follow in their tracks. That way the snow would be more packed for us, so we set up the trail shortly after daylight disappeared, but the moon came up so that helped.

We walked from three o'clock to eleven. We stumbled, we tripped, we fell, we got slapped in the face with the brush and were cut and bleeding and suddenly out of the darkness, there was the cabin standing in the moonlight. This is the first time anyone had seen them since 1939. I believe there were three or four of them in all. All of the doors were broken by the bears, most of the windows were broken and they were impacted with snow.

We picked one and wanted to light a fire but the stovepipe was full of frozen snow. We removed the stovepipe and knocked the snow out of it but then we had no fire wood. We broke up some pieces of furniture and lit a fire with them. There were several cots in the room but the mattresses were torn, probably by squirrels. It was a complete dirty, filthy mess but it was shelter. We stood around the stove and warmed up some. Then they opened the bag with the food in it. They took out a loaf of bread, a quarter pound of butter, one can of Dole pineapple chunks and that was it. Why would somebody pack this combination in one bag? The only conclusion we could come to was that there was another bag that was lost when the dozer went down and the cook couldn't get everything into one bag. The CEO decided that the food should be kept for an emergency. Nobody said anything and I waited for a few minutes and finally said to him, "What do you think we are in now? You can do whatever you want but I am going to eat my ration" and Carl said, "Me too."

Here was the person that got us into this situation we are in, and now he was going to tell us how we were going to die. We split up the food and we all ate it. I slept between what was left of two mattresses, fully clothed and when we woke up the fire had long died. I told the CEO to get his ass out of bed and find something to light a fire with. I think at that point he realized the danger he was in. I really believe any one of us could have put a bullet into him and have no qualms of conscience. Actually we would be able to justify it to ourselves and believe it would stand up in any court in the country. It proves that even though we had been civilized for generations, civilization is really only skin deep.

The only thing that was accomplished as far as I could see is that we did verify that the gold field did exist and where it was located. Now, if we could somehow manage to keep ourselves alive in those temperatures with no food, we would be very lucky. We left there and started following the trail that we had made the night before. We knew that it would lead us back to where the dozer sank and from there we would have the dozer tracks. Thank God, it hadn't snowed and wiped out our tracks.

After several miles, the mechanic said, "I can't make it; I just don't have the strength." We certainly were not prepared for this. We replied by saying, "What do you mean you can't make it? You have to make it. We have no choice. You have to keep moving. We all have to keep moving or else we will all die here. That's the only choice there is."

Some time passed and he kept walking and then he fell on his knees. He said, "Please leave me, all I want to do is go to sleep. Please just go and leave me here, I will be OK. I need to sleep." We told him that he couldn't lie down in the snow, and if he did, he would be frozen to death in less than thirty minutes. We told him we have no time for this, just get up off your knees and start walking with us and if you fall, get yourself up again and keep moving. We told him, "We are not leaving you and you are not leaving us, so cut the BS and keep walking." This went on for the remainder of the day and all night and the day after we stumbled into camp. All four of us were more dead than alive, but we had survived. After some food and some sleep, we were as good as new.

All through this period, the CEO was completely quiet. We knew he was scared of our reaction to his poor judgment. I really believe that he knew that if he stepped over the line that he would be in danger. I was totally convinced that if we survived, my career would be over. You don't tell the CEO of a company that has mines all over the globe to get his ass out of bed and get a fire going and also point out to him that he didn't recognize an emergency when he saw it. I really judged him all wrong. He was a bigger man than I had figured him to be. When he was leaving, he shook my hand and said, "Thank You" – nothing more and nothing less was said. Anytime that he visited a camp that I was in after that, he would make a point of finding me, asking me how I was doing and if I needed anything. I never saw or heard of the Master Mechanic again.

They radioed Fairbanks to put three or four guys on a plane that was coming to pick him up and when they landed at our camp, they took dozer number fifty five with them when they went to see if they could get the other dozer out by winch. It took them a few days to salvage everything. I often wondered if there was a bag or a box of food on board. I will never know. The episode was never again discussed. Carl and I bunked in the same cabin and we never spoke a word to each other about it. It was like it never happened.

The Athy Wagon and dozers number fifty five and number seventy three were returned to our camp. I have no idea of what was involved in the rescue. The plane returned and picked up the guys and returned them to Fairbanks. We stayed on working even though the weather was absolutely freezing. The only time we were able to freight the dredge parts was when the river and ground was frozen because freighting was all hauled on sleds.

Every night we were happy to return to our cabins and get warm by the pot belly stove. One thing that really stuck in my mind was what happened to our boots each night. The snow was so dry in Alaska that it was like sand. The reason was that as the flakes fall through the atmosphere, each flake is frozen and becomes an independent pellet.

When we walked into the cabin, some snow would come in with us and from the heat of the stove, it would melt. During the night, the fire would go out and the water that was on the floor would freeze. Each morning the sole of our boots would be frozen to the floor. We actually had to keep a log of wood nearby to hit against our boots to break them away – they were frozen solid.

The boots we wore were called "Bunny Boots". The U.S. Government had them designed for the troops that would be going to areas where they would be in sub-zero temperatures. They were the most remarkable boot you ever saw and to look at them you would question how they did the job they did.

They were made in Australia – the inside where the sole of your foot was, looked and felt like a felt insole that you would put inside your shoe and it was the same consistency. Underneath that was a very thin protective plastic sole, which was your protection from the snow. The upper looked like white canvas – nothing more. They were so warm it was unbelievable, but they could only be worn where the snow was absolutely dry. If the upper part got wet, it just fell apart. One day we worked eight hours outside and the temperature registered fifty eight degrees below zero and our feet were relatively comfortable.

We remained in Hogatza until late Nov. and were we ever happy to return to Fairbanks.

CHAPTER 9

Once we got back to Fairbanks I went back to 303 Minnie Street and was able to stay there for the rest of the winter. One day I was walking down the street in Fairbanks, I once again bumped into that great guy that I met the first day I arrived in Fairbanks. He was very glad to see me. He mentioned that he had often wondered what had happened to me over the past five years.

We sat and talked for hours and he said, "You know what you should do now with your experience? You should join the Operating Engineers Union. It is a very powerful union and you could work anywhere." I said, "I am sure it is but I'm sure you need connections to get in and I don't have any." He said, "You sure do." I asked him who I knew and his answer was, "You know me – I will take you to meet the Business Manager and I think I can get him to accept you. In fact, let's go over there now and see if he is in his office."

Off we went and he was in his office. He introduced me to him and told him that I was a wonderful guy and that I would be quite an asset to his organization. The guy said, "OK, if you are recommending him – that's good enough for me." I was signed up that day and became a member of Local 302 of the Operating Engineers. He later told me that he and the Business Manager were old buddies for years and he, himself, was retired from that union. What a gentleman he was.

We were total strangers and yet he took me under his wing on my first day in Fairbanks when I accidently sat down beside him on a bench five long years ago. I didn't know where he came from and I never knew his last name and now I cannot remember his first name. I never saw him again but I never forgot him. To this day I feel bad that I never properly thanked this wonderful person. I don't think I ever even bought him a cup of coffee. I'll never know why he took such an interest in me.

Because I was now in the Operating Engineers Union, I got a job working that winter at Ladd Air Force Base. They were enlarging the base and adding on landing strips. I operated a compactor; that's a machine that pounds down the gravel to make a base for the blacktop. That prevents the surface from settling after it is paved. We had to be certain that there weren't any bumps on the landing strip. I stayed there until it was time to return to Hogatza in March.

On March 17th, I went to company headquarters and from there we went to the airport and got on a Bush plane and headed back to "No Man's Land". I was so happy to be back with my friends and the peace and quiet, only broken occasionally by the howl of a timber wolf or the horrendous screech of an eagle. The quiet is so deep you can actually feel it. That is peace.

The Bush pilots are the greatest. The places that they fly to and the things that they do and the places they land, you would have to be more than a little crazy to do it. They don't live to a ripe old age, many of them crashed in Alaska and neither the pilots nor the planes were ever found. The others kept on flying. In the summer time they would land on wheels if there was any kind of a strip to land on, or else they would land on pontoons on the river, and when there was snow on the ground, they would land on skis.

Landing on skis is the worst landing because there are no brakes and when the skis touch the frozen snow, the plane takes off like a rocket and keeps going until it runs out of momentum or it gets tangled in the under-brush, which indeed will stop it. It is not a comfortable feeling, when you hear the noise outside and then when you take off again you have to help grab the plane by the tail and help pull it out of the bush and turn it around. On one ride there were four of us plus the pilot, with all our gear in the rear of the plane and we were supposed to land and he couldn't get the nose of the plane to point down, because there was too much weight in the rear. There was no way that he could get the plane down so we had to move to the front as far as we could and climb on each other's backs to push the nose down.

A buddy of mine was coming in over camp one day and the engine started to sputter and spit. Then the pilot said, "Oh, I forgot to open the valve on the other fuel tank." By the time he said that they were skimming over the tree tops, but they landed safely.

The "Big Four" are back in the same camp that we were in last year -- Carl, Ralph, Ernie and I. Nothing had changed. Carl did tell us that the barge would be arriving any day and the first shipment of dredge parts would be on it. Also coming was a large hut for a mess hall and several cabins, all of which had to be assembled. More workers were being sent out here so the first thing we had to do was freight the buildings to camp and have them ready when the crew arrived.

Our job was to excavate the lake to get water to it so that the base of the dredge could be assembled. We had to get the ground thawed with steam which would keep the guys busy and later we had to haul all the parts from the landing sight. Most of that would be done starting late next fall and all next winter.

A few weeks after we got back the natives arrived. They moved their wives and children and their sled dogs to their new campground. At the same time the barges arrived. Our first job was to unload the barges and send them back to Fairbanks.

At this point, we assembled the cabins for the natives. We did this at the dock so that they could remain with their families until we completed the construction. Then they were transported to the camp site. The mess hall would be assembled at the camp site. This was a large structure, as it had to accommodate forty people and transporting all the parts and assembling them was very time consuming, especially since the heating, plumbing and electrical work had to be connected. All the tables and benches had to be assembled also.

One Sunday morning we were working on the river bank when we spotted a little boat coming up the Koyukuk River. As the boat came closer, we could see a man and a little dog. The little dog was standing up on the bow enjoying the breeze. He pulled in and climbed up the river bank and introduced himself. He had a French name and was a Catholic Missioner. He told us his parish extended from the Arctic Circle North. The entire region was his territory to cover. He asked if there were any Catholics among us. There were three of us.

He asked us if we would ask the cook if he would let him use the mess hall to say Mass. We asked him if he had said Mass already that morning since it was Sunday. His comment was, "Is today Sunday? I don't even know what day of the week it is."

The cook said that was fine with him and Father said Mass and even gave a long Sermon. The interesting thing in a situation like this was, we were so out of sink with the world in general that you almost wanted to laugh at the whole thing. It wasn't that we were being disrespectful, we just were totally removed from the outside world and it just struck you as being stupid. It wasn't reality, as far as we were concerned.

This year was quite different than the last one. Last year we had three or four major projects that consumed all of our time. They had to be completed one way or another. Now, it was more relaxed. At least everyone knew what they were doing and where they were going. That wasn't how it was before. It was a whole different set of rules. One day you were doing plumbing work, another day electrical and maybe the third day carpentry or welding. You never knew what tomorrow would bring.

The natives had moved into camp which was approximately thirty miles from the women and children. They would be working at the gold field this season, not at the landing sight as they did in the past.

The cook got a new bull cook to help him keep the fires going and assist with the necessary work around since there were many more people here this season. I thought to myself, if they keep this up, this place will look like someone actually lives here. It was really beginning to shape up.

We were kept busy clearing the rest of the area and getting the roads completed before we started working on the dredge. Eventually we started securing the equipment and shutting down the camp and packing our huge wardrobe that we owned. Other than the sleeping bag, I could have packed everything into a large paper bag. I was wearing everything that I owned, because in those temperatures, you had to have good equipment and be well protected. The temperature had been in the fifty degrees below zero range for some time now.

Finally, we were ready to leave and were waiting for the plane to arrive. Ralph was all excited and he couldn't wait to get to Fairbanks and get himself a bottle of Old Bush Mill. He had told me long ago that he was an alcoholic and that was the reason the company sent him out there – that was the only way they could keep him sober. Every year when the work ended, he went back to Seattle and the only time he got sober was when he ran out of money. I asked him what he did when he ran out of money and he told me that he went to the Mission and then he panhandled.

Every spring the company sent him a ticket and he arrived back in Fairbanks and went to work. He was the only person that they sent a ticket to. He was the most brilliant mechanic in the whole company. There was nothing in the world that he could not do. He wouldn't change his lifestyle for anything. He always said that there was nothing better than a bottle of Old Bush Mill.

He asked me what I was planning on doing and I told him that I might go to Ireland again to visit my mom. It had been nearly five years since I was in Ireland. I'd see when I got to Fairbanks as I wasn't really sure what I was going to do. He asked me if I would be coming back to Hogatza and I told him that I intended to. He said, "Then you will be passing through Seattle, so look me up at the Mission on the way back." He told me he would definitely be there so I should stop and see him.

We arrived in Fairbanks on a Saturday night and the company picked us up at the airport and took us to their camp in town. Ralph didn't even enter the building – he headed for the first saloon and didn't show up at all that night. The next day I went looking for him and found him so drunk that he didn't know where he was. With my friend, Johnny Yogas, we put him in the back of the car and drove him out to the airport. There we bought him a ticket to Seattle and put him on the plane. The following spring, he told me he had no idea of how he got to Seattle. When he woke up he was there. I never told him how he got there. Drunk or sober, he was the most valuable employee they had. He was a great guy.

CHAPTER 10

I left a few days later and flew to Seattle/Tacoma International Airport. I was not quite sure what I was going to do at that point. I had a cup of coffee and decided that I would take a train down the coast to Los Angeles, spend a day there and then take a train to El Paso, Texas. I did that and decided to go across the border to Juarez in Mexico. What a hellhole. The only people that spoke English were the cab drivers and they wanted to take me to cat houses, and kids were on the street selling the services of their mothers and sisters. The women were sitting on the roadside nursing their babies. I spent one day there. That was more than sufficient. I left there that evening. I got another train and traveled across the south to New Orleans. It was so hot and humid that I thought I would suffocate.

I decided that I should go to Florida and visit my Aunt Kathleen – my mother's youngest sister. She lived in West Palm Beach. I spent a week with her and we had a lot of fun. She told me that I was an embarrassment and she didn't want to sit next to me at the beach. She said that I looked like an "Albino", my skin was so white. I told her I was really sorry but where I came from there wasn't much opportunity to get a suntan. She was quite a character.

I thought I was going to die with the heat. I just couldn't stay awake. It completely exhausted me. I made up my mind while I was in Florida that I would go to Ireland. I took a train from West Palm Beach to New York. It was a twenty four hour ride and when I arrived in New York, I visited the Campions on 175th Street in the Bronx. I stayed with them. Their son, Ed, was in the Navy so they gave me his room. It was the tiniest room I was ever in. When I went to bed my feet used to rest on the window sill.

I think we spent the whole week talking. I booked a passage on the same ship I traveled on five years earlier, the M.V. Britannic III, which was part of the Cunard Line. I hadn't seen Maureen in nearly five years. She had been writing to me all during that time – in fact she was my only contact with the lower forty eight states.

She was beautiful and such a kind person. Actually, even though we had hardly seen each other during all those years, we probably knew more about each other's life than anyone else did. We really were good friends and made a date to go out when I returned from Ireland.

I was really shocked at all the changes that had taken place in the city in that five year period. Neighborhoods that were really nice before I left were now so bad that you would be afraid to go into them. I went to 140th Street and Willis Avenue to visit my old friends. I rang the doorbell at one of their apartments and an African American lady answered the door. Every single one of my friends had moved out of that neighborhood and I was never able to locate them again. I didn't contact any of my relatives as I hadn't heard from them in years. I had paid my uncle long ago for the money he lent me to come to the states. So many changes took place in such a short period. I was shocked at what happened to everything – the music, the dances, Rock and Roll, Elvis Presley, whoever he was. I saw the hoola hoop and I had never heard of it. I had no idea as to what it was.

Remember I said that we had arrived back in Fairbanks on a Saturday night? The next day I was strolling down Second Avenue and I passed by the only theatre in town. I decided to go in and see the movie and didn't bother to look at what was playing. I sat down and waited for the show to start and I almost fell out of the seat. I was looking at Ireland – the movie was The Quiet Man with Maureen O'Hara, Barry Fitzgerald, and John Wayne. It was like reliving my childhood. I especially loved the music from the theme song—The Isle of Inisfree. When I was on board the ship going to Ireland, it was the first time I heard them sing the actual words of the song over the intercom system. It's a beautiful song.

After five and a half days, I arrived in Cobh, in County Cork, on the southern tip of Ireland. As we approached Customs, a gentleman came out and with a piece of chalk put a check-mark on each piece of luggage as it came down the row. That meant it cleared Customs. That was fine until he got to me. He asked me if those bags were mine. I had five bags because I had things that I had accumulated over the years that I had in storage and didn't want to leave there. He told me to open them and he turned them upside down and lifted the case off of each one so that everything was scattered all over creation.

He went through everything and at the end told me that I could put it back, it was OK. I asked him what he had been looking for. His answer was, "Dirty magazines, guns and ammunition." That was the rotation and I told him I was sorry to disappoint him. I don't know why he singled me out. This time I didn't fall for any "God Love You or God Bless You." Once was enough.

I decided to call home from Cork to tell them that I was in Ireland and that I would arrive home later that day. I didn't say how I was getting there – I took the train and arrived at the station, which was about a mile from our home. I left my luggage with the station master and walked through town and into the store only to see a man stretched out on the barroom floor having a heart attack. I recognized him and there were several people around him with a lot of commotion but they seemed to have everything under control, so I walked down to the kitchen and found mom. She looked wonderful and it was great to see her. I must say she had aged but still looked very good. She didn't know what was going on in the bar and I didn't tell her. Mike Daly did survive.

New York wasn't the only place that had changed, I hardly recognized the country and even our home wasn't the same. It was a complete shock to me – the only ones living there were Mom, Kevin and Eamon. Maureen and John were in the states, Chris was working as a nurse in England, Anita was in Nursing School and Catherine was studying in a Domestic Economy School. This was a far cry from the last time I was home when the eight of us were together for Christmas dinner with mom.

I went to church on Sunday and saw one person that I recognized. I used to serve Mass in this church and I probably knew ninety five percent of the congregation. This was the saddest experience --- I felt like I could cry. People would come over to me and shake hands and welcome me home and I had no idea who they were. Some of them I hadn't seen since I left eight years ago.

I really wanted to visit the farm to see what changes had taken place there. Even that had changed, not physically, but the whole method of farming was completely different. The equipment that was used for survival was now abandoned and rusted. I ran my hand over the rust and memories came flooding back. I remembered the horses that were so much a part of my childhood and were probably the most loyal friends I had at that time – they were long gone and replaced with tractors. I was sorry that I came, there were so many memories that I didn't want to think about them. I went to visit my grammar school teacher, who lived across the fence from the farm to find their house was now being used as a stable with nobody in sight. I had no idea what had happened to the family. That trip was like a nightmare and yet in a way it was a pleasant form of melancholy.. It was very sad.

When I got home, I inquired what had happened to Miss O'Beirne and her sister and her husband. The house was now a stable. Mom said that Bridie O'Beirne got married and built a new house. She asked me if I had seen a house next to the gate by the farm. There was a house that wasn't there before but I didn't know who owned it. Mom told me that her sister and her husband built a new house also on a different location on their farm. I went back sometime later to visit my teacher but she wasn't home and I never did see her during that visit.

One day a neighbor stopped in to visit mom and told her that the house next door where his three aunts had lived was being put up for sale. The last of his aunts had just died and he asked mom if Malachy would be interested in buying it. Mom told him that she really didn't know what I was doing or where I was going, but she suggested that he talk to me about it. His name was Fred Jackson – I had known him all my life. He came to see me one evening and we sat by the fire in our dining room and he asked me if I would be interested in purchasing the house and the land around it, which was approximately two and a half acres and just outside the village there were twenty one acres of farmland which would be sold with it.

Mom had told me that he was going to talk to me about it so I wasn't surprised. I also knew that mom loved that house and the orchard and the gardens. The orchard had one hundred and nineteen apple and pear trees, gooseberry and blackberry bushes and all kinds of exotic plants. His aunts had spent their lifetime working in the gardens and it was absolutely magnificent. I was familiar with it as I grew up next door to them.

I had thought about it after mom mentioned it was being sold and I figured that one of those days Kevin would be getting married and taking over the business and it would be very nice for mom to have a place of her own next door. I also thought the time was coming for mom to get away from the business world – she had spent her life working. After Fred and I discussed price, I bought the house and gardens and the twenty one acres of farmland. I had no intention of staying in Ireland at that time. I thought that maybe one day I might want to come back here but I really doubted it.

It really was very quiet there; there really wasn't anything to do. I did spend quite a bit of time with my cousin, Patsy Donohue – we were really very good friends always. I used to go visit my aunt and uncle that lived nearby and also an aunt and uncle on my father's side once in awhile or go into the town of Roscommon or Athlone once in awhile just to keep busy. I still had no interest in the grocery store or the bar.

About two weeks after I arrived home, I received a letter from a girl I went to school with. She was home on vacation and someone had told her I was home. She worked in Dublin and was the Private Secretary of the President of Ireland who at that time was Sean T. O'Kelly. Her name was Kitty Kelly – no relation to the President.

In her letter she said she would like to see me and I was shocked because she was my first love but I had never asked her for a date. I guess I was shy, I really don't know why. I was delighted to see her. I don't think I had seen her since our school days. She was more beautiful than I remembered her. We saw each other almost daily for the remainder of her vacation and continued in Dublin until I was getting ready to return to the states. Before leaving, I proposed to her and she accepted and I told her I would send her a ring from New York when I got there. I actually told her that I had a date with Maureen Campion when I returned and I intended to keep it. I told her that she had been a wonderful friend and had been writing to me for years and assured her that there was nothing to worry about.

For my return to the U.S., I again purchased a ticked on the M.V. Britannic III. That was the last time I sailed on that ship and she made her final trans-Atlantic crossing in 1960. It was a rough crossing but I enjoyed the company of the other passengers and we had wonderful entertainment. When we docked in New York, I was shocked to see Maureen and her friend Lizzie Keenan waiting to meet me. I hadn't told Maureen that I was getting engaged and I don't remember when I told her. She had told her mom that she had a date with me and her mom told her, "He won't keep it" and Maureen's answer was, "Yes, he will." Her mom laughed at her and told her that there is no way Malachy is going to show up and her mom said, "I bet you a quarter he won't show." Maureen said, "OK, I bet you he will."

Maureen won the bet and when we got back to their house that night, her mother paid the quarter. I took it back to Alaska with me; had the quarter dipped in gold and had a ring put on it to make a charm for Maureen's charm bracelet as a reminder of our first date. Maureen has that charm to this day.

The day before our date, I went to Brooklyn to visit my sister Maureen, who had gotten married while I was in Alaska. I asked her husband, Bill if he knew of any reputable jeweler as I wanted to buy a ring. Bill brought me over to a friend of his and I purchased a ring for Kitty Kelly. Maureen told me later that I let it slip on our date that I had been to the jewelry store in Brooklyn and she figured it was to buy a ring for Kitty Kelly. She knew I was dating her from my letters to her while I was in Ireland.

On our date, we went to the movies at a little theatre on 174th Street and Boston Road called the Dover. Then we went to an ice cream parlor and sat and talked for a long time. I don't think it was about anything in particular. It was just the way we had been talking to each other over the past eight years.

Suddenly I realized how much my "little friend Maureen" meant to me. I said to myself, "You idiot, you have been in love with her all those years and you didn't even know it. Boy what a mess I am in now." Of course, I didn't know what her feelings were. She never indicated anything to me. We were just great friends and have always been.

I did stay at Campion's house that night and slept in Ed's bed once again and would be heading back to Alaska in a few more days. My head was swimming – I knew I had to come to some conclusion in the next few days. Should I mail the ring or not mail the ring? I couldn't say anything to Maureen and I surely couldn't ask her what her feelings about me are. This was one situation that I had to resolve with myself first. They are two beautiful girls and I am in love with both of them. What was I going to do??

I didn't know what Maureen's feelings were but if I had a choice, which one should I choose? I went for a long walk in Crotona Park to ponder this once in a lifetime decision. Dear God, please help me to make the right decision. Maureen was who I decided was my choice, if I had that choice.

That night we went out again and I told Maureen I was in love with her and to my delight, Maureen told me she was in love with me also. That made my decision much easier. I still had the ring in my pocket, so the next day I returned the ring to the jeweler in Brooklyn.

A few days later, I said good bye to Maureen and all the Campions and left for Fairbanks. We promised we would write to each other every day and we did.

CHAPTER 11

When I arrived in Fairbanks, I shopped for the necessary essentials needed to last for the next six months.

This year they asked me to go to Gold Stream Camp. Carl Johnson told me he wasn't returning to Hogatza Camp either. He figured we had paid our dues there. He told me that in a few weeks he would have a nice job for me in Chatanika Camp. The camp was located about thirty miles north of Fairbanks.

I was back in Gold Stream and my old friend Danny Loren asked me if I would like to take a few days off before I left for Chatanika Camp and go along with him and another guy for a road trip. He said we would like to see if we can get to Dawson in the Yukon Territory. He said his Ford van was in good shape but we had no idea what the road conditions were. I called the Fairbanks police to inquire about the highway and they said, "Don't even think about it" but they did suggest we call the State Highway Commission for their advice, which we did. They said the same thing as the police chief. The highway is passing through a very remote region in Alaska. If anything goes wrong, there is no assistance available from anywhere. "Be advised, do not attempt it."

You would think that any normal person would have listened to those messages, but no we decided we were going to Dawson. Early the next morning, Danny and his buddy, whose name I cannot remember, and I climbed into the old Ford van and started on our way. We soon found out that the highway was little more than a trail and the farther we traveled the worst it seemed to be getting. We bounced along over the rocks, the roots and the potholes but we kept going. Some of the time we were down to five miles per hour and suddenly we came to a complete stop. The engine was running but we were standing still.

We had snapped the drive shaft and we were dead in our tracks two hundred and seventy five miles into the Alaskan wilderness. We had no idea how close we were to the Yukon/Canadian border. We also had no idea how far Dawson was from the border. We learned later that if we had gotten to the border, Dawson was still seventy five miles away and we were twenty five miles from the border. At the time all we knew was that we were two hundred seventy five miles from home and we had no idea how close the Yukon Territory was.

We did realize that we were sitting on the brink of the Yukon River and the mosquitoes were eating us alive. In our hurry to leave, nobody thought of bringing fresh water, sleeping bags or food with us. With the warnings we were given, you would think something would have registered. We were stupid, beyond stupid. We did find a can of pork and beans that must have spilled from a bag of groceries so that was our food supply. We did have the Yukon River for water. It took some time for the seriousness of our situation to sink in. By scanning the horizon to try to make some sense as to which way we were going to escape, off in the far distance we saw smoke rising towards the sky. As the day progressed the cloud grew larger and larger. We figured it must have been a forest fire.

A little while later we heard a noise coming toward us which sounded like a car or a truck. It was a jeep with a guy in it and he stopped and introduced himself, as Ranger Joe from the Forest Rangers. He said he was on his way to investigate the fire that was burning in the distance. He looked at our problem and told us that we were lucky that he had come by because if he hadn't, he didn't know what would have happened to us. He told us we could have been there for weeks and not be seen by anyone.

He told us he would take us with him to Tok Junction which is far south of Fairbanks and we could hitch a ride from there to Fairbanks but only one would go back because the other two would go with him to the fire. He said he would need all the manpower he could find. One of us could return to Fairbanks and report where the other two had gone to. He told us we should decide which of us would be returning to Fairbanks. He suggested we pull straws to decide and I won. The others didn't get back to Fairbanks until a week later.

The law is when a Ranger needs you, you have no choice. You must go, no matter who you are and nobody can do anything about it. We were extremely lucky that he found us. I am not sure we could have survived. Our faces and hands were so swollen from the mosquito bites. Even our eyes looked like they were sunken in our faces. I got a ride with a truck driver back to Fairbanks.

I moved to Chatanika Camp before they returned to Gold Stream Camp. When I arrived in Chatanika, I didn't have any idea what I was supposed to be doing. It didn't take long for me to find out. Carl Johnson found me and said, "Come with me, I want to show you something." He brought me out to an area of the gold field where there was a huge crane. I had never seen such a monstrous piece of equipment. He asked me if I thought I could operate it. I said to him, "Are you kidding -- what would I know about a monster like this?"

He said it was just delivered and he thought I could learn to operate it. I asked him what made him think that I could possibly do that and he said, "Look, this thing doesn't even have wheels or tracks." I asked him how it moved. He told me it doesn't need wheels or tracks, it walks and it covers seven feet with each step. He did tell me what a great opportunity it was for me to learn this machine and that he knew that I could handle it.

He told me that he really needed an operator and asked me if I would be willing to do it. I told him that if he needed someone and he thought I could handle it, then I would definitely give it a try. His answer was, "I know you will do fine so come and let me show you the inside of the cab." It was a huge five cylinder Fairbanks-Morse diesel engine. To reach the top of the cylinder head, you had to climb up two sets of stairs. The crank case was so huge, you could walk inside it. That was the main engine and there also was a large gas engine driving an electric generator supplying power to the controls – not to mention the gears, the drums, the cables, the air tanks, etc. He told me that I would have an oiler who would take care of the oiling, the greasing and the cleaning of the equipment and this was my seat behind the control panel.

He said there would be three operators, each working an eight hour shift and that we would rotate every two weeks. The machine would run twenty four hours a day, seven days a week. I asked him what we would be doing and he told me that the bedrock in this field was very deep and the dredge cannot dig that depth so we had to remove anywhere from ten to twenty feet of gravel. They were in the process of installing a conveyer system that would carry away the excess gravel which would be dumped about three quarters of a mile away.

The conveyor would be fed through a hopper which we would keep supplied with gravel. The bucket in the ton weighed fourteen tons empty and it held six cubic yards of gravel. You could drive a car into the bucket. I would be in charge of the crew and they would man the stations on the conveyor system.

What Carl didn't tell me was that a day earlier, a mechanic who was working on the machine told them that he was able to operate it. When they needed a truck load of gravel, the truck driver backed the dump truck into position for him to load it and the mechanic swung the full bucket of gravel over the truck-- he wasn't able to hold the load on the brakes and the full bucket crashed down on the truck. Luckily the driver had left the cab. They said the truck looked like a sardine can. Now, wasn't that encouraging news? I hoped Carl knew what he was doing with an expensive piece of equipment at stake.

I must have gotten instructions from someone but I have no memory of it. Things must have gone OK as the next thing I remember was getting into the truck with the crew and no supervision on the graveyard shift from midnight to eight in the morning. I really enjoyed operating the machine. I went eight hours without speaking to a soul. If there was someone speaking, you couldn't have heard them anyhow. Bobby Hudler was one of the other operators; he came from South Carolina.

We decided to move out of camp and about a mile from the camp there was an abandoned mining village. I would say there were six or seven houses in it but nobody was living in any of them. We examined each and decided on a log cabin. We moved in and it was really in good condition. We did clean it up a little bit and the first night after we went to bed the humming of the insects started. It got louder and louder to the point where you couldn't stand it. It appeared to be coming from the walls. The next day we moved out – the problem was that the seams between the logs were stuffed with moss and the insects were living in there. They were there by the thousands.

We went house hunting the next day and chose a new residence that made us the town's governing body. Bobby had a car so we could go to town and do our shopping. The main reason we moved out of camp was because of our hours. We couldn't sleep with the noise during the day and we couldn't eat when it suited us and we could walk to work through the woods. It was a little uncomfortable walking through the woods in the fall when it was dark. Sometimes I worried that I would meet a bear walking in the opposite direction.

One night, I thought someone was playing a trick on me but I couldn't imagine who it could be because there was nobody near where I was. As I was walking someone would say boo and when I stopped, it stopped but once I started walking again it would start again. It was a bright moonlight night and eventually I spotted an owl perched on the very tip of an evergreen tree. He was perfectly framed in the circle of the moon. When I would move, he would hoot, hoot but I thought he was saying boo, boo.

There was a little trading post with a post office. It was the Chatanika Post Office. One day Bobby and I were standing outside the trading post and we were watching a cloud of dust, which meant that a car was approaching. The highway wasn't paved and the dust from the gravel could be seen for miles. It turned out to be a pick-up truck and it stopped. A man got out of the driver's side and a native lady got out on the other side. She was none other than the wife of the guy that owned the Galloping Goose River Barge who had run the trading post in the tent village on the Koyukuk River.

She was the lady that never went to school but taught herself to read and write from reading the labels on the cans and the boxes. We were so glad to see each other. I never thought that I would see her again. This was the same person that wrote me a letter when I was in Gold Stream Camp and I was able to understand what she was writing about. She told me that she had left her husband because he gave away the last baby they had, without ever discussing it with her. I didn't ask her if the guy she was with was her new husband or a friend so I don't know who he was. I was just so glad to see her and we never saw each other again.

Years later, our daughter Maura gave me a book to read while I was on vacation with Maureen in Florida and the title of the book was, "On the Edge of Nowhere" by Jim Huntington. It was a story of his life in Alaska. This is the same Jim Huntington that owned the barge that freighted the materials to Hogatza from Fairbanks on the Koyukuk River. His wife ran the trading post on the banks of the Koyukuk and I used to visit her there. Of course she was the squaw who told me that she had left her husband because he had given away her last baby without discussing it with her. I wish I had saved that letter.

I had met her again at the Chatanika Trading Post hundreds of miles south of Huslia and then I am reading in his book in 2008 – fifty years later – that he had no idea of why she walked out on him. I could have answered that for him. I worked with him and his brother, Sidney, and most of the Athapaskan tribe in that region.

Anyway, that was a very quiet winter – Bobby Hudler and I worked different shifts and sometimes only saw each other when we were relieving each other at work. We worked seven days a week – each of us took an eight hour shift and rotated every two weeks. My favorite shift was the swing shift (four to midnight) because on that shift you got some regular sleep and still had time off during the day.

Thank God for Maureen – it gave me reason to go to camp to get the mail and come home and read her letters. Then I would write back to her and either go back to camp or town to mail it. This gave me something to do.

CHAPTER 12

The main talk of the town during this period was the upcoming vote on statehood. It was interesting to hear all the different conversations – the majority of the adult population was against it, because they liked it as a territory and didn't want to see it change. The young people, however, were all for it becoming a state. Eighteen year olds were eligible to vote which meant most of the high school seniors and all the college students were most likely to vote for it.

I personally voted against it, but obviously my vote wasn't sufficient to make a difference. I left that fall, between the period of the election and the actual signing of the treaty declaring Alaska the 49th state.

One day before the voting took place, I was in Fairbanks and went into the jewelry store to buy Maureen an ivory bracelet which came from the tusk of a mammal that had been extinct for millions of years. It was very pretty and I knew she would like it and she still wears it over fifty years later.

While shopping there, the jeweler showed me a 14K gold charm in the shape of the state of Alaska with the number forty-nine in the middle of the charm. He told me a limited number of these were produced. He commented that if Alaska doesn't become a state, this would be a collector's item and if it does, it still would be a special memento because there were such a small number of them available. I bought one to add to Maureen's charm bracelet. I figured she could use something to keep her mother's quarter company. She still has both of them to this day.

When the season ended, the company that I was working for offered me a job on a survey crew. Back in 1912, when the U.S. surveyed the territory they had placed markers there. These were the markers that we were looking for in 1958. It was essential that they be found in order to set up boundaries. We had the maps indicating where the markers were supposed to be, but the problem was finding them. When we did, they were iron rods driven into the permafrost and on top was a brass disc which had engraved on it, "Department of Interior" and the date 1912. They had never been located since they were originally placed until we found them forty six years later. Maps were drawn from these markings so it was very precise.

During this time we visited every camp in the area. The guy I was working with had the most incredible eye of anyone I have ever known. He could spot a rock with gold specks in it from ten feet away. Every day he would pick up some rocks with gold in them and put them in the back of his pickup truck.

That summer he dug the foundation of a house and over the years he had collected enough rocks to put a complete basement in with those rocks he had collected. He finished the basement and put in a fireplace and covered it with a temporary roof and insulation and lived there for that winter. He had plans to finish it the following year. Every rock in the basement had gold in it – It was very, very unusual. The only thing I ever picked up was five gold nuggets from one of the gold mines. I don't know what happened to four of them but I do know that Maureen still has the one I gave her. She had an eye put on it and wears it on a chain around her neck. She's often asked what it is when she wears it.

His wife was the justice of the peace and constantly told me that she would perform my marriage, free of charge, if I wanted to get married in Fairbanks. However, I didn't think it would pay for me to fly Maureen up for a free marriage. It was easier for me to return to New York.

When the snow and ice arrived, that was the end of our surveying. I figured I would return to New York and see Maureen and ask her if she wanted to get engaged. If she said yes, I would probably remain in New York. I didn't know for sure if I would be returning to Fairbanks or not.

I met one of my friends and he asked me if I would be leaving for the lower forty eight for the winter and I said I was. He told me that he and a friend were leaving on Sunday and were driving and I was welcome to come along with them. They were going to Kansas and could drop me off in Hutchinson, Kansas. Now, remember I was the guy who said that never again would I drive this, but when they offered, I said yes. Some people never learn.

On Sunday morning we left Fairbanks. It was very cold – fifty degrees below zero. We planned that with three drivers we could drive non-stop except for food and fuel. We expected to make good time. The weather had other ideas. Shortly after we left Fairbanks, a light snow started to fall and it worked itself into a blinding snow blizzard. That's what it had reached by the time we reached the Alaska/Yukon border about midnight.

I didn't think the Canadian Customs Inspector was in a very good mood. Perhaps we disturbed his sleep. He wanted to know if we were all born in the states. Stupidly, I said no. He should have asked if we were all Americans, and then I would have answered yes. Now he wanted to see my passport. I told him it was in the back of the station wagon in a suitcase and I didn't know where it was among the stuff. I told him I had other ID that I could show him and asked him why he had to see a passport that was in a bag in the car in a blizzard. He told me, "It's like this; if you want to pass through here you are going to show me a passport, blizzard or no blizzard."
So, we had to empty out the station wagon until we found the right suitcase and the passport. There was not another person or car to be seen anywhere except a snow

plow which we followed for miles and miles. If it weren't for the plow, we wouldn't have been able to drive at all.

This was just the beginning of a nightmare trip. We passed through the blizzard moving very slowly and sometime the next day we came to a bridge. As we approached it, the entrance was very confusing. The blinding snow had obliterated almost all visibility. The road and the bridge were one white blur. I was driving at this time and we were almost halfway across the bridge and the next thing we saw was a car with flashing lights coming up behind us and pulling us over.

The policeman wanted to see my driver's license. Then he walked around the car and he kicked the ice and snow from the license plate. The car had Alaskan plates and I asked him why he pulled me over. He said I was speeding. I said, "Speeding?" I wasn't doing anything more than twenty five miles an hour." He said, "Yes, I know but the speed limit is fifteen miles per hour." He said, "You know I can bring you guys in and you will have to wait three days for a justice of the peace to come into the area. I will have to lock you up until then."

All three of us started to laugh – first of all we couldn't believe that a Royal Canadian Mounted Police would say such a stupid statement. He asked, "Did I say something funny?" All three of us said at the same time, "Why don't you bring us in? You would be doing us a big favor in this weather. We are sure you have a nice warm cell and a bed to sleep in and the food would probably be pretty good." His answer to that was, "Get the hell out of here." We did find out later that we were in a super, secret area. It was a secret Royal Canadian Air Force Test Base.

Sometime later, we went off the road in a skid, and we missed going over an embankment by as little as a few feet. Had we skidded any further we would never have been found. We couldn't even see the bottom; someone was really looking over us. The elements really threw us for a loop – snow and ice and when we got further south, we got hit with hail and then fog. It took us seven days and nights to get to Kansas and I don't believe I slept for a single minute and I don't think any one of the others did either.

All I remember was being dropped off at a railroad station in Hutchinson and boarding a train on the Santa Fe line to Chicago. The next thing I remember was being shaken awake by a guy saying, "For Christ Sake, Mac, don't you ever wake up?" Apparently he got on the train with me and twenty four hours later I had not woken up. I had to change in Chicago to the New York Central line to go to Grand Central in New York.

I was sitting on a bench waiting for the train when I suddenly started to shake. I didn't know what was happening to me. I really thought I was going to die. In fact, I was convinced that I was going to die. It was a good thing that the train didn't arrive while this was happening and eventually it passed, whatever caused it I don't know.

CHAPTER 13

I got an apartment on Vyse Avenue, which was just off Tremont Avenue in the Bronx. I lived with the Grahams, who were friends of the Campions. Joe had just retired from the New York City Transit Authority. He worked in the garage repairing buses. They lived on the fifth floor of an apartment building and Joe had not gotten accustomed to retirement yet. He just did not know what to do with himself. He was a very nice person but I really had to laugh at his antics. He would get up for breakfast and then he would walk down five flights of stairs and go to the candy store and buy the newspaper. He would come back home, climb five flights of stairs again and might read the paper for a half hour and he would be off again. He would walk down the stairs again and stand on the sidewalk and look up and down the street and stay there for awhile and go back upstairs again. This would go on all day long – up and down, up and down. It was really quite sad to watch him.

Joe was quite short and his wife was quite tall. They were such a lovely couple and made me feel like I was part of the family. One morning we were having breakfast and I was sitting facing the window looking at the apartment across the court yard. There was a lady washing the windows and she was wearing a house-coat but didn't bother to button it and she was very, very well endowed. I was enjoying the scenery and I wanted Joe to enjoy the view so I pointed her out to him. When Joe looked over at her, I thought he would fall off the chair. First he turned beet red and then he started to choke. His wife jumped up, she thought he was dying as she had no idea of what was happening. He didn't want her to see the view so he wouldn't tell her what was happening and of course, I acted totally innocent. That was some breakfast – especially the dessert.

Maureen's dad told me that he found a job for me in a deli downtown. I don't remember exactly where it was located but it did a huge sandwich business in the Wall Street area. He said the salary would be good and they wanted me to start the next day. I really wasn't particularly interested because I just couldn't see myself making sandwiches in a deli or anywhere else but I didn't want to hurt his feelings so I said OK. He gave me an address and I went there the next morning.

Wow, that was an experience. It was like a sandwich factory. The people were lined up two deep and this went on all day. I couldn't believe what was happening – what kind of a world is this? I just can't imagine how anyone could live and work in this environment. Well the day ended eventually and I got out of there and went home and never even went back, even to collect my pay. I really learned something that day and that was that the retail business and I were parting company and that was it – never again.

I did thank Maureen's dad for his help but I decided that was not for me. He asked me what I thought I would like to do and I really didn't know but I was absolutely sure what I was not going to do. He couldn't really understand how I could feel that way. He had worked in the grocery business his whole life and made a very comfortable living. He said it was very secure because people have to eat no matter what. I didn't say this but I thought to myself that they are going to do it without me. I was not really in a panic at this time because I knew I could return to Alaska in the spring and live there but I didn't know where Maureen stood on this. I did have time to see where this was going.

A friend of the Campions was a Superintendent for Real Estate Corporation offered me a job in a building that he was in charge of as a handyman. The building was located on 108th Street where Broadway and West End Avenue intersect. It was a very nice building and the tenants were really nice. In a short time I knew most of them from doing repairs in their apartments. Stu was the boss – that was the only name that I knew him by. I did a lot of repairs in the building and eventually I was taken to other buildings the company owned to do some work and Stu had to drive me there and pick me up and bring me back to his building.

Stu and I got along very well but one day he told me he was going to have to let me go as he couldn't afford me in his budget. I said that I understood and told him to do whatever he had to do. I asked him if I should leave that day or complete the week and he asked me to please complete the week. About two or three days later, the owner of the corporation came in and he said to me, "I just wanted to tell you how sorry we are that you are leaving us. It was great having you here and we will miss you and wish you didn't have to leave." He wished me lots of luck. Apparently Stu was getting nervous. He was afraid that I was going to take over his job so he made up the story about him having to let me go and I guess he never expected the big boss to show up, so he told him that I was quitting. I said nothing to the boss as I didn't want his job and I didn't want to get him in trouble because he was a good friend of Jerry Campion.

During this time, Maureen and I dated steadily and around Thanksgiving we started to talk about getting married. I felt the proper thing would be to ask Jerry if it was OK with him that I marry Maureen. His immediate response was, "No way". I told him that was OK, I would go back to Alaska and that would be the end of our romance. I knew it would be fine with Maureen's mom for us to get married. The very next day Jerry called me and told me he changed his mind and gave us his blessing. What I didn't know was that Maureen told him that she would go back to Alaska with me and we would get married there.

We got engaged on Christmas Eve. In those days in the Bronx, if a girl went to midnight Mass on Christmas Eve wearing a corsage, everyone figured she had gotten engaged. Maureen was the first one in her crowd to get engaged so there was lots of excitement among her friends. The wedding plans started and we picked the date of Oct. 3, 1959, to get married.

Max Pollack, a City Plumbing Inspector lived next door to the Campions. The day after I finished working with Stu, he asked me if I would consider a job with a plumber. He said he had a lot of connections with them as he inspected their work every day. Two days later, Mrs. Nellie McGuire, the owner of The Cantwell Plumbing Company, hired me as a plumber's helper.

I was teamed up with Rolf, a rather stern individual. He always reminded me that he was the mechanic and I was the helper, as if I didn't know. We got along very well most of the time. He had a wicked temper when things didn't go well. When something would break, he would go into a wild rage. He was a nice guy but he wasn't a very good mechanic. We would be sent out on a call – usually in an apartment building and I think that everything that went wrong was on the top floor.

When we parked the truck Rolf would insist on taking two pails of fittings that weighed at least fifty pounds each up the stairs. When we didn't know what the problem was, I used to ask him why we didn't go up and find out what we needed first. His answer was always that we couldn't waste time coming down to the truck to get the fittings we needed. By the time I hauled those pails of brass fittings up five flights, I needed oxygen.

One day we were sent to an apartment building to install a new basin in the bathroom. As usual I had to haul the famous pails up the stairs and then I had to go back down for the basin. Rolf hung the basin on the wall and proceeded to connect the hot and cold water lines onto it. I was sitting on the edge of the tub watching him and I asked him didn't he think he should install the trap on the sink first before hooking up the water lines. He once again asked me, "Who the hell is the mechanic?"

He continued to connect the water lines and then asked me to hand him the trap, which I did. Then I sat back down on the bathtub edge and waited. He started to screw the trap onto the waste line and found out it could not be done because the sink was in the way. It had to be taken down in order to screw the trap onto the waste line. Now he had to disconnect the water lines and take the basin off the wall in order to install the trap. That was what I tried to tell him in the first place but helpers do not tell mechanics how to do the job. He flew into a rage and he stood up and kicked the two pails of fittings, spilling them all over the bathroom and onto the living room floor. He then told me to pick them up.

I was still sitting on the bathtub and I did not move. Then he screamed at me – "Didn't you hear what I said?" I told him that I heard him loud and clear but the fact is that I was not going to pick them up because he kicked them over and he was going to pick them up. I asked him were we going to leave the job without all the fittings and have the tenant pick them up when they came home. I told him the decision was his and reminded him that he was the mechanic and it was his responsibility to make sure the job was completed and that the apartment was left neat and clean so he should do just that. He had to pick up every last one of the fittings and I sat there and watched him. He never pulled that one again.

In a short time, I found myself being sent out to jobs on my own. One day I was somewhere in Manhattan and when I finished with the job; the truck was nowhere to be found. I didn't know if someone stole the truck and I kept walking up and down the street. I then started to wonder if I parked it somewhere else. I could have sworn that I parked it on this block but I started walking around the neighborhood and after about an hour, I found it about three blocks away. Somehow or other, Manhattan and I don't seem to get along very well.

Not long after that I was handling assignments alone. I felt I deserved a raise. When I asked for a raise and I was told "No", I told them I would work that day but that would be my last day. That evening when I got back to the shop they told me they had changed their mind and I would get mechanics' pay. I remained with them until sometime after Maureen and I got married. Nellie McGuire and Rolf and his wife were at our wedding.

During that time I was learning the trade. Most of the work was called jobbing plumbing. Not much new work; mostly repair and replacement. You never knew what you were going to run into next.

During our engagement I asked mom if she would come to New York for our wedding. She had not been back to the states since she left in the twenties. Maureen had gotten married to Bill Byrnes and they were living in Brooklyn. By this time Maureen had two children and was expecting her third so we convinced mom that she could be here to help Maureen out with the baby and also be here for our wedding. We were shocked when she said yes.

Mom arrived around the first week of Aug. and Kathy Byrnes was born a few days later. None of us thought about how hard the heat would be on mom. Between the mosquitoes loving her and the heat killing her, we really thought she would be on a plane back to Ireland before Oct. came but she held out and loved being here for the wedding.

John was in the Army and arranged for leave to be my Best Man. He arrived the day before the wedding just in time for the rehearsal. It was quite a shock for him to meet so many people all at once and be in a wedding within a few hours.

Oct. 3rd, 1959, was a beautiful day. Back then weddings were in the morning at a Mass. Ours was at 11am, followed by a reception at Blazes' Reception Hall in the Bronx. I'll always remember when my brother John stood up to give the toast – he was so nervous that he said, "I'd like to propose a toast to Malachy and" – the next thing he went blank. He quickly turned to me and asked, "What's her name?" Of course that was heard by everyone over the microphone. We've laughed about that many times over the years. He did feel better when one of the priests at the wedding that was a friend of the Campions for years whose name was Father O'Donoghue walked over to John and told him the same thing had happened to him – only he had forgotten his own sister's name when it came time to give a blessing. Nerves can play tricks on you.

We went to Fort Lauderdale, Florida on our honeymoon. While down there we visited my Aunt Kathleen and her husband, Jim Worden in West Palm Beach. Jim insisted that we bring home a palm tree that was growing out of a coconut for our new apartment. Can you imagine us coming off the plane with a two foot high palm tree that we placed in the waste paper basket from the hotel bathroom in order to be able to carry it? We carried it onto the plane and the crew asked us where we got it. They thought it was beautiful. Aunt Kathleen often wrote and asked us, "How was Jim's nut doing?" It lived for years in the bathroom of our apartment.

We also spent an afternoon visiting Maureen's cousins; the Crowleys. Sis and Jim and their four children previously lived downstairs from the Campions and Maureen babysat for Jimmy, Michael, Brian and JoAnn. We had a great day on the beach in Hollywood, Florida. They were the best and we are all still close friends today. We continue to visit them in Arizona and they visit us in New City.

We returned to our apartment at 893 Crotona Park North in the Bronx. This was across the street from where Maureen grew up and we spent many very happy years there.

Right after the holidays in 1959, Max, the plumbing inspector, stopped over to the apartment one evening and asked me if I would consider changing jobs. He knew I was happy in Cantwell Plumbing but he had a good friend that needed a plumber to work with him and he thought we would be a perfect match. His name was Jack Elliott and he worked mainly in Westchester and Rockland Counties. Most of his business was in Automatic Lawn Sprinkler installation and repair.

The thought of getting out of the city and not have to work in apartment buildings sounded very appealing and after meeting Jack one evening and hearing what he had to offer in salary and working conditions, I knew he and I would do great together.

The first day I worked with Jack we were on a call somewhere in Westchester County. He apologized for the fact that he was so quiet. He said he wasn't much of a talker and he didn't want me to be offended. I told him that was OK with me because I wasn't a great talker either. We were a great pair; any normal person around us would think we were mad at each other. Sometimes we would work for hours, side by side and not a word would be spoken. Not only was he a great boss but he became a wonderful friend.

He owned a yacht which was kept at the Stepping Stone Yacht Club located just near the entrance to the Throggs Neck Bridge. Actually, the bridge was just being built at the time and we sat on his boat and watched them connecting the first cable that connected the steel towers. George Stenderhoff, Sr. owned the yard and he had hired Jack to do some plumbing work for him at the boat yard.

One of the jobs was to install a new hot water tank in one of the buildings. Jack left me to do the installation while he went to give a customer an estimate. When he returned I was still there but the building I was working in was gone and so was the hot water tank. What happened was I was soldering some water lines using a propane torch and the next thing I knew, a lady driving down the highway saw flames shooting out on the eve of the building between the wall and the roof and she came flying in to ask me if I knew that the building was on fire. The lines were located too close to the plasterboard wall and something ignited inside the wall. By the time the fire department got finished, not only was the fire out but so was everything else. I guess accidents do happen when you play with fire. Nothing was ever mentioned about this again.

Maureen and I spent many Sundays on the boat with Jack and his wife Florence. The boat slept four and had all kinds of cooking facilities and Florence loved to cook. The only problem was when you finished eating all the food Florence made; it was very difficult to stay awake. We took many a nap on that boat. They were wonderful to us.

Jack was Catholic but every Friday he would order a meat sandwich for lunch while I had cheese or fish. He used to tell me that it was a good day that you can get a nice meat sandwich, and he didn't care what the Church thought. However, on Good Friday he wouldn't touch a meat sandwich and he would say, "No way will I eat meat today because it is Good Friday and nobody should eat meat on that day." When I would ask him why it was OK to eat meat on the other Fridays, his answer was, "They don't count." Jack liked his own rules better than those set down by the Church.

We had a lot of fun and we would be asked some of the strangest questions by his customers and we would keep a straight face and give some nonsensical answer and often, they would say, "Oh, gee I never realized that's how it works.."

Jack would pick me up every morning and we would head off to do whatever jobs he had scheduled and when we returned in the evening, he would come up to our apartment with me and we would each have a bowl of soup before he went home. We had our own little routine going.

I really enjoyed working with Jack and I found the work very interesting. I probably would have stayed working with him forever, but one Sunday morning in March of 1961, I met Mike Doughan outside St. Thomas Aquinas Church. Mike knew that I had worked as a crane operator in Alaska and asked me why I wasn't doing that now. I told him that I had no connections with Local 14 of the Hoisting Engineers in New York but I was a member of Local 303 in Seattle, Washington which covered the territory of Alaska. I did tell him that I had my New York City License.

He told me that he also was a crane operator and was working for his brother, Martin, who owned his own crane rental company and he would speak to him about giving me a job if I was interested. The next day I got a call from Martin that I could go to work for his company. I really felt bad leaving Jack but felt this was an opportunity that I could not let go by. Martin got me a permit to work for Local 14 of the Operating Engineers.

This was a whole new experience. The machines were like toys in size compared to the machines that I was familiar with in Alaska. Actually you could pick up the whole machine and put it inside one of the buckets of the cranes that I had worked on. They were more dangerous because they were subject to tipping over very easily, especially when you were operating with a hundred and fifty foot or two hundred foot boom, but you got used to it and I learned to work with them. I was sent to operate a crane at St. Luke's Roosevelt Hospital on 59th St. and Amsterdam Avenue placing steel for Iron Workers. Little did I know then that our granddaughter, Ella, would be born in that hospital forty four years later.

It was a hair raising experience because huge steel beams had to be hoisted up and swung over taxi cabs, cars, buses, and pedestrians and one slight mistake and who knows how many people could be killed? After this job was finished, I was sent to Lincoln Center, which was being built at that time on 65th Street between Columbus and Amsterdam Avenues. That was less congested and we had more room to operate.

When we finished there, I was sent to the Bronx when the Cross Bronx Expressway was being connected to Bruckner Boulevard – in the West Farms area of the Bronx where the exit was under construction as part of the project. The Bronx River runs through the area, under the Metro-North Railroad. Alongside the railroad tracks are the high powered electric lines that supply power to the tracks.

My friend, Eddie Brady, studied with me for the AMPES License – which means Any Motive Power Except Steam. This was considered the most difficult New York License to obtain and was the only New York City license that it was illegal to print any material pertaining to previous tests or any other information. This license was required to operate a crane in New York City and the only information available was from people who had taken the test and they only told you what they could remember, which was usually very spotty. So all the little tidbits would be gathered and given to the guys who would then share them with each other.

When the information was given to you, a promise had to be made that you would return the papers to the person that gave them to you by the next evening; with no excuses. Eddie got them and passed them on to me. Maureen would take them to work the next morning and my brother John would go down to 43rd Street where Maureen was working and bring them back to me to get them back on time.

The copying equipment that was available at that time was very difficult to operate and very slow to make copies. The copies were "wet copies" and you had to wait a certain amount of time for them to dry and then pull apart the negative from the copy and go on to the next one. After a certain amount of copies were made, you had to change the liquid that the copies went through and this was a major project. Maureen would go to work very early in the morning before the machines would be used by the secretaries and get all the copies made before nine o'clock. John would go to her office on his way home from work (he was working nights in Brooklyn) and pick them up. We had quite a system going.

The test was a horror. There were five distinct parts to it. It covered any type of engine – gas, diesel, electric, air compressors, types of cables and what purpose each could be used for. Fifteen hundred people took the written and we never knew how many people passed it, but those that passed it had to take the Practical Exam, which turned out to be the most nerve wracking experience that I have ever been through.

The test was given on the docks; somewhere in Queens. That morning there were five of us scheduled for the test. One of the inspectors stood in the middle of our little circle and explained what was expected of us. He said he would pick one person at a time and that guy would go through each phase and then he would be asked to leave. Originally, there were five of us and all of a sudden, I realized there were only four. What happened to the other guy? Where did he go?

We were so engrossed in his instructions that nobody realized that someone left. The inspector looked around and asked us, "Who is missing? What is his name?" Of course nobody knew because we were all strangers to each other. Now there would only be four taking the test that day. It was a very large area and all kinds of earth moving equipment and a large crane were parked on the bank of the sound where there was a huge river barge docked and it was loaded with gravel.

The first man was picked and he was taken to a large construction air compressor on the far side of the lot. The only nice thing about that equipment was that you didn't have to climb up on it to operate it. Although there are safety controls, the high pressure creates a potentially hazardous situation. Mishaps have resulted in fatalities. This equipment was mostly on safety controls, how they function in the different stages that the air went through and the devices protecting each stage; the more stages; the higher the pressure.

The next after that was a D8 bulldozer with a blade. When I saw that I knew that this wasn't just talk about all the different parts and controls. This was one you were going to have to operate. I had to push gravel and spread it on a road – I had no problem with that because I had been a CAT Skinner for a couple of years in

Alaska. That was what they called bulldozer operators. The next one was a crane and this was the most nerve wracking. The inspector climbed up on the crane and stood behind the seat and I had to explain all the controls and their purposes. Then he said, "Start up the machine" which I did and then he told me to move the machine into position and I want you to unload the gravel from the barge.

At that point, I froze. I was sitting behind the controls with one hand on the lever and looked up at the top of the boom, which was about one hundred and fifty feet in the air with the barge full of gravel floating in the sound. I heard the inspector say, "Pick up the bucket and swing out over the barge – then drop the bucket and fill it will gravel – hoist it into the air and swing it ashore and dump it." He finished with his instructions and I was still sitting with my hands and feet on the controls and not able to move. He waited, I didn't move as I was fighting to get myself under control. I kept telling myself not to do anything until you control yourself so I sat and he waited and I was getting a little calmer. I finally said, "OK, OK."

The next thing I heard was, "Well are you going to move?" I answered him by saying that I am now OK and I did just fine after that and was able to do exactly what he wanted. After that came the operating of those large rollers that you see on the highway. For me that was the easiest part.

The first guy seemed to have done well until he came to the last part, which was the easiest one. I saw him climb up and start moving. They had set up an obstacle course with those cones that you had to manipulate through. Well he lost control, flattened out most of the cones, continued on, completely out of control and slammed into a row of parked cars. I have no idea how much damage he did. I felt bad for him. Apparently his nerves got the best of him.

Of the five that started out – one disappeared altogether – I became frozen for a period sitting behind the controls of the crane, but I did pull it off. Another smashed into a row of cars and I don't know how the next two did as they came after I finished. Thinking back on this, I can easily understand that out of the fifteen hundred that started out taking the written exam and we never knew how many passed and were allowed to take the practical, how only 15 licenses were issued.

Eddie Brady and I were two of the fifteen that passed and he went to work running a crane on the Bruckner Boulevard Interchange at West Farms in the Bronx. The crane was located on a strip of land between the railroad tracks and the Bronx River. Eddie got off the crane one day to talk to someone and one of those sudden storms with wind gusts and heavy rain started and Eddie saw the boom starting to turn towards one of the high tension wires. He had forgotten to put on the house-brake. The wind gust caught the boom as it was turning toward the power lines. He started to run to stop the turning crane just as the rain started pouring down. They say he got to within twenty feet of the crane when the boom crashed into the power lines. The current traveled down through the crane into the wet ground and through Eddie and killed him instantly. There was an oiler on the crane and nothing happened to him. The next day Local 14 sent me to replace Eddie on the job. That was one of the worst experiences of my life.

My first day on that job I was placing those large rocks on the side of the riverbank to keep them from washing away but first a foundation of crushed rock had to be laid on the bottom of the riverbed. This was followed by large boulders that covered all the sides of the river banks. This work was done at low tide because at high tide the river depth was increased by approximately five feet. I had no experience with working under water. When the tide went out, the crew wanted to lay the base for the next section. I had to change from placing rocks on the banks to handling buckets of crushed rock.

When they had the bucket installed I swung the bucket over and filled it with rock – swung the crane out over the river and had to boom real low in order to reach where they wanted me to put the rock under water. The further down the boom is lowered, the greater the weight load increases. I was well within the limits -- weight wise when I lowered the bucket of crushed rock into the water. Surprise, surprise, the water poured into the bucket of rocks and doubled the weight. The crane started to tip sideways into the river. Luckily I released the brake in the nick of time; otherwise, the crane and I would have been in the river bottom. I worked there until the job was completed.

The job ended during Christmas week and I figured I wouldn't worry about it until after the New Year since no jobs would be starting that week. New Year's Eve night 1961, Maureen and I were at a party and I met Pat Conway who was a good friend of Maureen's mom and dad. We were sitting talking and he asked me how I liked running cranes in New York City. I said it was OK; a very stressful job but it was fine. What I didn't like about it was that jobs were constantly ending in one place and starting somewhere at a new location. You never knew where you would be working tomorrow. It could be in Manhattan today; Coney Island tomorrow; Long Island a few days later and that was what I really disliked about it.

He said the he knew that I had worked as a plumber. He was a steamfitter and since there was not much difference in the two trades, he asked if I would be interested in getting a work permit in Local 638, the Steamfitters Union. He said that he would tell the Business Manager that I was his nephew and he was pretty sure they would give me a permit. He told me it was a very powerful union and the salaries were very, very good. I said, "Sure, I'd love to give it a try. If you could get me a permit, I would be very grateful." He told me that it might take him a few days and he would get back to me.

Sure enough he called me a few days later and told me that he had gotten me the permit and that he would pick me up the next morning because I was assigned to the same job that he was working on. The next morning, my "new" Uncle Pat picked me up in his new, shiny white Chrysler and drove to Tinton Avenue in the

Bronx where there was a new housing development going up. There were five – twenty one story buildings in the complex.

"Uncle Pat" took me to the Steamfitters' Shack where you changed to your work clothes and everyone sat around talking until it was time to go to work. I was introduced to everyone as his nephew. The foreman said, "Your partner is Bill." I learned that there was a rule of the union are that no steamfitter can work alone. You must have a partner; why I have no idea but those are the rules and they were followed to the letter. I really loved the job.

It was all brand new work and certainly much easier than jobbing plumbing where you would be sent to an apartment building anywhere in the city and you never knew what to expect when you got there. It could be a leak under a sink, or water dripping from the ceiling which meant it wasn't in the apartment you were sent to but in the apartment on the floor above. Sometimes a bathroom wall had to be opened in order to get to the leak. Dismantling beautiful work didn't make you very popular with the tenants.

With the Steamfitters, you didn't have to deal with all those unknowns. It was such a pleasure -- it was like night and day. Partners were assigned to a floor. The job was to install heat convectors in each room. They had to be attached to the wall and the steam lines had to be connected to the unit and the return lines from it. There was an official quota as to how many units were to be done in a day.

I had a problem. The problem was that Bill, my partner, would leave the shack at eight a.m. – go to our assigned floor and by ten a.m., he would say that he was leaving. He told me that if someone came looking for him I was to tell them that he just went up to one of the other floors. "Don't worry about it" were his parting words.

This went on every day. He lived somewhere in upstate New York and he just went home. I didn't mind because I was able to get the required quota completed by about two p.m. and would spend the rest of the day pretending to be busy. This went on for months.

The foreman must have known what was going on but for some reason, he ignored it. The work load had been done so he didn't care. The real kick in the head was when the foreman said to me, "Donoghue, how many units are being installed in a day?" I told him nine units and he asked if I was counting just connecting the steam supply line to each unit. I said "No – the count is connecting both supply and return lines." He said each man was distinctly told to make one connection. That means you connect one line to each convector and you have connected both the supply line and return line. So you are doing double what everyone else is doing. I understood that one a day meant units completed. So he told me that I understood wrong and had to stay within the rules like everyone else. Bill left every day at ten a.m. and I had been able to complete what I had been doing before two p.m. Now, under the new rules, I had enough work to keep myself busy until about eleven a.m. so that's about three hours of work. This was the system and you couldn't buck it so you spent your time pretending to be working.

One afternoon the owner of the company arrived on the floor – he introduced himself and asked where my partner was. I told him he was here a few minutes ago and he must have gone up to the floor above for something. He said nothing else and left. The very next day, he arrived again and once again asked for my partner and I told him he just missed him and once again he said nothing and just left. The next morning I told Bill that the owner has been here two days in a row looking for you so you better stay on the job as I am sure he will be back again today. He said "F--k him" and went home again and sure enough the owner arrived back again. He asked me the same question again so I stopped working and I looked him in the eye and I said, "What the hell do you want from me?" He didn't answer – he just turned and walked away. When the day ended and I went back to the shack, the foreman handed me my pink slip and had another one for Bill to give him the next morning. I was the innocent victim but the result was the same. I never saw Bill again.

CHAPTER 14

I had been working on a permit in Local 638 since Jan., 1962, and in March I was called to join the B Local called the Metal Trades Branch. I went to work for the Kirby Saunders Company. This time I was working in the shop and this was a very different situation. Here we did only fabricating. Each person was given a blue print of a floor and every piece of pipe that was needed for heating and air conditioning was shown on the print and the type of fittings required. The pipe ranged from one and a half inches to four inches in diameter. The readings had to be taken from the plans. The precise cut was made and properly labeled. The exact location and the spot that it would be installed in had to be printed with paint. There was no room for error. The finished pieces were shipped to high rise office buildings in Manhattan and were picked up by a truck and delivered to a job site and each bundle was delivered to the exact floor where the steamfitters installed them.

We did have wonderful equipment to work with. During this time I was attending Metropolitan Trade School at night. The reason I started going to school was to help my brother, John. I had gotten him a job in Local 30 in the Operating Engineers Union through my very good friend, Bill Tracey, who was the Business Manager of the Union. Bill got John a job as a mechanic's helper in Fanny Farmer's Candy Factory in the Riverdale section of the Bronx.

John's mechanical experience was practically nil and he worked under a chief engineer and a few weeks after he started, the chief put him on the evening shift, but he was the only one in the Engineering Department at night. He would tell John what he wanted him to repair. Most of the repairs were on steam lines and plumbing lines that were leaking. John wasn't familiar with these types of fittings, wrenches, pipe cutters, etc. so when everybody went home John would call me and tell me what the chief wanted done.

I would tell him what materials he would need, the type of wrench that he needed and describe the fitting required and explain how to do the job. Night after night he got his work done and gradually he was able to take care of more and more on his own, but one thing he needed in order to keep his job was a Refrigeration License, for which he would have to go to school and study.

The problem was that school was in the evening and he couldn't get away from work to attend class. I told him I would go to school and I could teach him what I learned; which I did. Actually, I had no interest in Refrigeration and had less interest in a license. I started off going to school and immediately became fascinated by the whole concept; really enjoyed the classes and I graduated. Everyone in the class was talking about sitting for the next test that came up for the license, so I said to myself, "What the heck, why don't I take the test just to see if I can pass the written? If I do, then I may as well take the practical and maybe even get the license."

John and I sat for the test and when we met after the test, John asked me what I thought of it. I said I thought it was extremely difficult and then I asked him what he thought of it and he said he thought it wasn't too bad. Gee, I'm the one that went to school and taught him what I learned and now he thought it was kind of easy and I thought it was very difficult. I figured I must be a much better teacher than I was a student. I was hoping that he would pass because he was the one that needed the license for his job. I didn't need it, so it didn't matter to me. Hopefully he would pass.

Of course many, many weeks went by before hearing from the city. Eventually one Saturday morning the letter with the results arrived in the mailbox. Maureen opened the mailbox and there were the two letters from the city. We argued over who would open his letter first. John finally said he would open his and he read that he failed. What a disappointment. Then it was my turn for the bad news so I very slowly opened the envelope. I passed. John had to go back to studying again. He passed on the next try. Then he was able to get a job as a mechanic at Bohack's and was qualified to operate the equipment.

I got a notice from the city that I was to report to the Bronx Terminal Market at one p.m. on a certain day. I was still working in the Shop in the Bronx. I went to work that morning but got permission to leave. I told them where I was going and everyone wished me luck. I took a taxi to be sure that I got there on time. It was a huge place. They supplied fish, fruits, and vegetables to most of the city's grocery stores. You can imagine what the engineering division was like with that amount of refrigeration required to keep it operating.

There was a group of five of us scheduled to take the exam and there were two inspectors. They gave us the usual pep-talk and told us we had thirty minutes to walk around the plant and examine the machinery that we would be tested on. We were warned that we were not allowed to speak to each other – and if we did we would be automatically disqualified. They told us if we needed to smoke to please go to the back end of the plant and the final request was that when the inspector spoke to you; please do not smoke in his face.

We had thirty minutes before the exam started so we went in different directions to look over the equipment. I saw one of the guys reaching into his pocket and take out a pack of cigarettes, a second candidate followed him to the rear of the building. The law clearly stated that you are forbidden to smoke anywhere in an ammonia plant. I tried to warn them by making eye contact and shaking my head no and whispered "Don't do it" but of course they couldn't hear me with the noise from the machinery.

We were told no conversation with each other so I couldn't risk speaking out loud to either one of them but I tried to warn them. As soon as they lit the cigarettes they were told they failed the test and to leave immediately. I thought those inspectors were real creeps but then, those guys should have known better. We were told at school they would do everything possible to get you annoyed so be very careful that you don't lose your temper, under any conditions. They are experts at getting under your skin and the reason they do it is to see how you react under pressure.

For the first half of the test both inspectors were with you – one played the bad guy and the other played the good guy. After the first few minutes of questions, the bad guy said, "Tell me something, where the hell did you go to school?" Sometime later he said, "If I asked you to start this machine and put it on line, how would you do it?" So I started to explain the required procedure because it was a long procedure since there were so many lines to be opened and closed. It was a maze of pipes going every which way. You have to remember all the steps – otherwise you could blow the thing apart.

After I was halfway through he interrupted me with another question. Now I had to stop what I was doing to answer his question and then he said, "OK, finish what you were doing." I started at the beginning again and he interrupted me again and I had to stop once more and answer his question. Once again, he told me to proceed so I went back to the beginning again. He did this three times and each time I would start at the beginning and this time, he blew up. "You have done this twice already, why don't you carry on from where you were?" I said, "I cannot get this finished unless you stop interrupting me and I am not going to risk blowing the plant up so please stop interrupting me." When I was about halfway through he said, "OK go ahead and finish what you were doing."

A few minutes later he asked me about something that was about fifteen feet up in the air among a maze of piping. I answered and he said, "Point at what you are talking about; how do I know what you are looking at?" I said to him, "Why don't you give me that pointer that you have under your arm and I can point to what I am talking about?" We were not on very friendly terms at that point. The nice inspector said, "If he didn't think you knew what you were talking about, he wouldn't waste his time talking to you" and I said, "Oh that is nice to know."

Things did not get any better. Finally it was over, "OK, you can leave through that side door over there." I said, Good bye and thanked them and just as I got to the door, one of them said, "We have one more question -- how many pounds of ammonia would you say is stored in this plant?" I said, "I have no idea how many pounds they actually store here but if they have more than two hundred pounds, they are breaking the law." He looked me and said, "Why the hell don't you get out of here?" I was more than glad to oblige. I walked outside and called a cab and left -- I don't know if I was more annoyed at them or myself and I was convinced that I had blown the test big time.

Several weeks later the letter from the city arrived informing me that I had passed. After all that, I actually had the License and I had no idea what I was going to do with it.

One day I received a call from John telling me that the chief engineer at Fanny Farmer's asked him if I would be interested in doing some work for him on weekends as he needed to repair and replace many high pressure steam regulators and steam traps and he would pay me union wages. John said he would talk to me about it and he would let him know. I told him, "Yes I would do the needed work but I wanted time and a half for weekends and if it was OK with him, I would require a helper." He agreed to those conditions, so every Saturday morning John and I would start working, but first we had to check out the candy.

There were rows and rows and rows of steel shelving and every shelf was filled with boxes and trays of chocolate candy everywhere. There was one particular candy that we thought was the greatest thing we ever tasted. It was half caramel and half marshmallow covered with chocolate; it was the best. The major problem was that every Saturday it was in a different location and we wasted a tremendous amount of time each week trying to locate that particular one. I felt like leaving them a note asking them to stop moving our favorite candy all over the place. It was costing the company so much lost time because no candy – no work. We really were like "two kids in a candy store". Little did I think that Mike and Robyn would own a co-op on this same block in Riverdale years later.

I stayed working in Kirby Saunders until New York Plumbers went out of business and Kirby Saunders had their shop in their yard so they had to close up also. The next day I went to a job on 158th Street and Riverside Drive. Two new buildings about twenty four stories were under construction. The first morning I arrived on the job, the steamfitter foreman welcomed me and the first thing he told me was that the company we were going to be working for was a New Jersey company and that they had no business operating in the State of New York and hopefully we would put them out of business.

I was surprised to hear such a stupid comment but was smart enough not to argue with the foreman of the job. I learned a short time later that his brother was the job superintendent. He brought me to the shack. On the construction site each trade had their own shack and that was where you congregated until it was time to start work and get your assignment for the day. No steamfitter was allowed to work by himself; contract rules dictated that steamfitters must work in pairs.

An old-timer was assigned a partner. He simply barked, "I don't want him" and the foreman said, "I didn't ask you if you wanted him or not. I told you that you are getting a new partner." The old guy said to him, "And I told you I don't want him" so the foreman said "You are getting a new partner and here he is" and that settled the argument.

We all went our separate ways and it turned out the old guy and his partner were working on a four inch pipe. When you were working on that size pipe, you used a forty eight inch wrench, which was very heavy. The old guy climbed up the ladder and when he got near the top of the ladder, he dropped the wrench and it fell on his new partner's foot and smashed it. He had to be carried out and taken to the hospital. The only comment from the old timer to the foreman was, "I told you I didn't want him as my partner."

A few days later the foreman handed me a blueprint and said, "This is a four inch steam return line -- start in the boiler room." The boiler room was about four levels below street level and these floors were for car parking. When we had piped in the boiler room and we came up to where the line came up through the floor to the next level, we discovered that the four inch line would be coming up in the center of the car ramp. I immediately went to the foreman and explained the problem and he looked at me and asked, "Is that what the blueprint shows?" I told him that it was and he said, "Well then there is no problem – that is where you put it." I said, "This pipe will go up through the center of each ramp" and once again he looked at me and asked, "Is that what the print shows?" and when I said that it was, he looked at me and said, "Put it there."

We wasted weeks installing this pipe through the four floors. When we got to the first floor and were installing steam lines and return lines, one set of pipes was right in the center of the window. This would be repeated in a straight line for twenty four floors. Completely in awe I went back to the foreman and told him we had another problem. This time I got a lecture. "Donoghue, is there something wrong with your brain?" I said that I didn't think so. He replied, "Well then why do you keep coming to me with your problems?" I said, "Maybe I have a conscience" and his answer was, "Let me explain something to you – you are getting paid to install those lines according to the print, and you will get paid to remove them and then you will get paid to install them again in the right place, so what is your problem?" After that lecture I never questioned anything, no matter how stupid it was.

Christmas time came and they were still pouring the floors with concrete. The company didn't give the concrete workers a party or even a bottle of liquor for Christmas, so they filled every opening that was for pipes, cables, water lines, steam lines, etc. with concrete. The Steamfitters didn't have to put the company into bankruptcy, the cement workers did.

The weather turned very cold and the building required temporary heat so the steamfitters would pick one guy to cover a shift and put some heat up. I was picked to cover the three pm to midnight shift and about eleven forty five p.m. my replacement came in and I had to climb up on top of one of the boilers to open a valve. I stepped off of the ladder onto scaffolding installed by the insulation contractors and the minute I stepped on the planking, which wasn't supported properly, it flipped me up in the air and I fell a story and a half landing on the concrete floor. I grabbed a gas line as I was falling and got spun around and hit the back of my head on the corner of a cement column. I hit the floor and was hurt. The guy who was replacing me called a cab to take me to the hospital.

I couldn't move my right arm – the back of my head was split open and I fell onto an oily floor so between oil and blood, I must have looked like a real mess. When I was being admitted, a nurse came with a pen and pad for me to sign some documents. I wasn't very nice to her and told her that if I could sign that I wouldn't be in the hospital. I spent five or six weeks out of work with my right arm, which was fractured in several places, in a sling.

I had to get up each morning before Maureen went to work so she could help me get dressed. I thought I would go nuts sitting around the house each day. Thank heavens for Maureen's mom who lived across the street – we spent many hours each day talking.

While shopping one day Maureen and I saw a picture that we thought would look good over our couch. I said to Maureen, "Instead of buying one, why don't I paint one?" She looked at me like I was crazy because my right arm was taped to my body but we bought some canvas and some oil paint and I spent the next several weeks painting with my left hand. Believe it or not, that painting hung over our couch for many, many years.

When I returned to work, the job was nearly complete. I came home from my last day at work and Maureen was still in the city. She didn't get home until about five thirty and I got home each day about three thirty. I cooked dinner each evening. That particular evening the phone rang and it was my good friend, Bill Treacy. We were talking about nothing in particular and he asked me how was work going and I said, "It's funny you should ask me that, I just finished my last day." He asked me if the job had ended and I said, "Yes". He said, "That's great". I asked him, what he meant; "Are you saying that it's great that my job ended?"

He said, "Maybe, now you will listen to me. How many times have I asked you to get out of construction and work for Local 30? You now have your Refrigeration License and I have a very good job for you. I'll tell you what, I will pick you up tomorrow morning and we will go for a ride." I asked him where we were going and he said, "It doesn't matter; you don't have to know, I'll see you in the morning."

The next morning, Bill arrived in his big Cadillac and he wouldn't tell me where we were going or what we were going for. He told me to just sit back and enjoy the ride. The next thing I knew we were crossing the Whitestone Bridge and I said, "Where the hell are we going now?" We were on the Van Wyck Expressway; again I asked him if he had any idea of where we were going and he told me that I asked an awful lot of questions. I agreed that I was but I also told him I wasn't getting any answers. He just couldn't understand why I couldn't just sit back and relax and enjoy the scenery.

Eventually we came to an area of local streets. He kept driving for awhile and finally stopped along side a building and he turned the engine off and said, "Well we are here." I looked around and I asked, "Bill, what are we doing here; where the hell are we; what is the name of this place?" He said, "This is Jamaica, Queens." I replied; "Well now I know that this is Jamaica, Queens but what are we doing here?" He said, "Do you see this building on your right? That is a meat packing plant that has been closed for about five years and was just bought by a new company. The owners contacted me because they need an engineer to activate the machinery and run the plant. They will open for business as soon as the plant is operational. Now does that answer your question?" I asked him, "What does this have to do with me?" He said, "I need an Engineer to open this plant and that is what I want you to do. You are licensed and I know you are capable of doing it."

I said to him, "Do you know what I think, Bill? I think you are out of your mind; you have completely lost it. Just look at these facts; I never saw the inside of a refrigeration plant in my whole life. The only plant I was in was the Bronx Terminal Market for my practical test and I know nothing about refrigeration plants. This plant has been idle for five years and can you imagine what kind of condition you can expect to find the equipment in?"

Bill had mentioned that it was an Ammonia Plant and from what I had studied, I knew that they were hazardous. The operation required very high pressures and very low temperatures. All I know was what I studied, I got a license; big deal. I said to Bill, "How you can consider putting me into this, knowing what I know, which is nothing, is beyond me." Bill looked at me and said, "I am not as stupid as you think; I am smart enough to know that you can handle this, which means I have more faith in you than you have in yourself. Now, are we just going to sit here in the car and argue or are you going to consider it? I have lots of men who would be delighted to get this job but I would really love you to take it and I know you will not regret it. Say Yes and I will have the keys for you tomorrow. If you want to start tomorrow you can and you will be your own boss – how about it?"

I said, "OK, I will give it a shot. Get me the damn keys and I will open the place up one way or another. Bill, you are not as smart as I thought you were." We were great friends but we never agreed on anything.

I did take the job and I truly enjoyed what I was doing. What was nice about it was that I was the only one working in the building and I wasn't under any great pressure. I was amazed at how much I was able to accomplish in a few weeks.

The owner, Joel Rubin, told me that he was so happy with the way I got the plant operating that I would never have to buy meat again. Each Friday evening as I was leaving work there would be a bag of meat waiting for me in the office. I never knew what was in it so it always was our Friday night surprise. It was only Maureen and I and they sent so much meat that we spent many a Saturday giving out meat to friends and family. One time we didn't even know what the meat was – it turned out to be a full Filet Mignon – neither one of us had ever seen this piece of meat before. Eventually we bought a freezer and had a wonderful selection of meat. This went on every Friday night until I left County Fair Meat Packing many years later.

Across the street there was a Shortening Plant, where they processed cooking oils and shortening. The Chief Engineer was Jim McKillop; a real nice guy and we became very close friends. He was very helpful to me. He had a Stationary Engineer's license but was never able to pass the Refrigeration test. He had taken the written test three times and failed each time so he was never able to get his Refrigeration License. His plant had an ammonia system for refrigeration and this required a license to cover the system. They asked me if I would cover their system with my license and they would pay me a salary each week for the use of my license. I would walk across the street a few times each day to make sure everything was OK. Now I was on two payrolls but I was also shouldering dual responsibilities. Jim and I continued to look after each other.

In April, 1964, the World's Fair opened and Local 30 supplied all the Engineers that were needed to keep it in operation. Bill Treacy called me again and asked me if I would be interested in an Engineer's job at the Fair. I told him that I had a job now that I put an awful lot of work into and as strange as it may seem, I really liked it. Now you want me to leave here and go someplace else. His answer was, "Would you please stop talking so damn much and just listen for a change? It would be an evening job if you are interested. Why don't you stop in at the Fair and see Pat Ferguson, who is the President of Local 30 and in charge of all the Engineers at the World's Fair. You know Pat and he asked that you stop in to see him so that he can offer you the four o'clock to midnight shift or the midnight to eight a.m. shift, whichever you prefer."

Since I finished my job at three o'clock, and was right nearby, I could easily start working at the Fair at four o'clock. I told him that I would stop in at the Fair on my way home that evening and have a talk with Pat. When I got there, Pat was sitting outside his office in a lounge chair in the sunshine. He pulled up another chair for me and we sat and we talked and talked about all kinds of things, except work. Eventually, he said, "What shift do you want to work?" I told him I would prefer the four o'clock to midnight. He said that would be perfect and I should stop in the next day after work. The paperwork would be completed and he would get my Entry Pass. My assignment would be the Hawaiian Pavilion. He told me he needed me to start the next day and to make sure that I brought my license with me.

This is the same license that I got a short time ago and at the time I was asking myself, "Now that I have this; what am I going to do with it?" Never did I think I would use it to cover three jobs in a sixteen hour period. Sometimes things happen in spite of you.

I arrived at the Hawaiian Pavilion and I believe it was the only pavilion at the entire Fair that you had to drop a quarter into to get in. There were four glass entrance doors and at each door was a beautiful Hawaiian girl with her arm full of leis, and she would place one around each person's neck and welcome them to Hawaii. The lobby was magnificent with a huge pool with waterfalls cascading down into it and behind it was a volcano. People used the pool as a Wishing Well. The amount of money that would accumulate there was mind boggling.

I arrived at the door and a gorgeous girl wanted to hang a lei around my neck, I said, "No thank you – I am looking for the Engineer's Office." She asked me if I was the engineer and when I told her I was, she replied, "Well let me give you a Double Welcome." She put two of them around my neck and told me my office was right inside the door. It was a very large office and the only thing in it was a desk and a few chairs and a file cabinet.

I sat down at the desk, not sure of what I was supposed to be doing and a beautiful Hawaiian girl breezed in who said, "Hi", and walked to the rear of the office and started to undress. Then came another girl; followed by another. Before long there were five or six of them all changing their clothes and sauntering around in their underwear talking and laughing as if I wasn't there. Eventually they were all changed into their traditional dress and were ready to go to work. They were all very friendly as they headed off to work and I realized this was how they routinely changed shifts.

Awhile later, the girls came back and began undressing and changing into their street clothes. I really thought that I must have become invisible but since they all talked to me, I knew that I wasn't dreaming or hadn't died and gone to heaven. Normally I would complain about all this activity and would have told them that this was an office and they would have to find someplace else to hang out but, I made a very difficult decision and decided to be a "Nice Guy" and let them continue doing whatever it was they were doing.

Well I had another surprise coming later – about ten p.m. they closed the front doors and prepared to lock up for the night and when the public had all left the building, I walked out of my office and saw standing in the middle of the pool three or four Hawaiian girls with their long Muumuus thrown over their shoulders and picking up the coins that were thrown into the Wishing Well. They were only interested in the quarters; boy that was some sight to behold. This was only my first day on the job and I had put up with all this "inconvenience" and I wasn't sure if I could handle all this pressure. I did survive; it wasn't easy but I rose to the occasion.

With three jobs going, I wasn't getting much sleep. I worked in Jamaica Monday through Friday and at the Fair I worked Saturday, Sunday and three nights during the week. At least it wasn't five double shifts in a row. I would leave home at six a.m. and start in County Fair in Jamaica at seven a.m. and work until three p.m. Then I would drive to the Fair and start at four and work until midnight.

Many nights the baseball game at Shea Stadium would end about the same time as the World's Fair and you couldn't move on the highways. I would be sitting in bumper to bumper traffic when I should be at home sleeping. Sometimes if I got home at one thirty in the morning I would be lucky and I had to be up again at five a.m. It kept me very well behaved – I didn't have the energy to get myself in trouble.

Maureen came out to visit quite often and she got to know the Hawaiian girls very well. They were nice enough to invite her to their "Big Luau" at the end of the season. This had been talked about for weeks and was the biggest event of the year in their eyes. They dug a hole in the ground by the edge of the lake and lined the hole with rocks and built a fire. It was a large opening. A pig was then wrapped in banana leaves. Chicken wire was placed all around him to hold him in place. They lowered the pig into the hole on top of the fire and then filled the hole with earth. I don't remember how long he cooked for but it was a long time and then everyone gathered around for the digging up of the pig.

Finally they were able to reach into the hole and pull out the banana leaves, and the wire that was holding the pig. In the process a piece of wire got embedded into one of the guy's hands and the blood shot all over the pig. Maureen was a little hesitant of this operation from the beginning but when this happened she lost whatever appetite she had and being pregnant did not help how she felt at that moment. She thought she was going to get sick in front of everyone.

The Hawaiians spoke of poi like it was candy from heaven. I took a small taste and I thought it was like wallpaper paste. Everyone had a wonderful time at the party and there wasn't a bite left of the pig.

One night at the Fair I was so exhausted that I couldn't keep my eyes open and I was walking around outside trying to stay awake. The outside was landscaped to represent the state of Hawaii; beautiful Palm Trees and tropical plants. They also had a large theatre where they had continuous shows and Hula dancing. This was located near the lake. During my walk I found myself at the rear of the theatre – between it and the lake and I sat down at the edge of the lake. Some hours later I woke up and both of my feet were in the lake with my shoes on. I looked up and saw palm trees and I was completely confused. I had no idea where I was. What came to mind was I thought I had died and was now in Heaven. Luckily I woke up before they closed the place up for the night. That lake is still there but, of course, the theatre and the palm trees are long gone. Every time I pass that region of Queens on the Van Wyck Expressway, I smile to myself and remember that night.

One night the air conditioning system went out of order and I was working on it trying to get it running again when a guy walked in and introduced himself. He said he was the supervisor for the company that had the contract for all the maintenance throughout the Fair Grounds. He asked me who I was and I told him my name and he asked me what my position was.

I told him I was the Engineer and he asked me what I was doing. When I told him I was working on the air conditioning unit to get it back in operation, he told me, in no uncertain terms, this was not my job but it was a job for the Maintenance Division. He then informed me that in the office was a manual which clearly told you that if equipment broke down, there was a telephone number that the Engineer was to call and was to request a mechanic to come out and repair the equipment. He told me that if he saw me again with a wrench in my hand, I would be out of a job. Wow, I thought to myself this guy really likes to show his power.

About a week after that I got a report that there was water leaking from the ceiling over the main entrance doorway. This was a serious concern because someone might slip and get injured. I went looking for a ladder in order to get up into the ceiling to see what was causing the leak. I figured it was from an air conditioning unit that was located above the doorway.

I put a few wrenches in my pocket and removed a few ceiling tiles and climbed up into the ceiling. There was no flooring, only the cross beams. The ceiling tiles were attached to them and in order to reach the area that I had to get to, I had to balance myself on the edges of the beams. I very cautiously stepped from beam to beam and just as I reached the area where the leak was, I slipped and came crashing down through the ceiling.

Luckily one of my legs got hooked over one of the beams, so here I was swinging with my head down over the Main Entrance Doors. I couldn't get up and I couldn't get down and there were broken ceiling tiles all over the floor. A lot of people came to my rescue; they had to first find the ladder and try to get my leg unhooked from around the beam and then they dropped me down – holding onto me so that I wouldn't come crashing down on the floor on my head.

When they got me straightened out; I went back up again and found the leak, repaired it and didn't call the telephone number that the supervisor had directed me to.

My other two jobs were coasting along very nicely, which was fine with me. I knew that Maureen wasn't too happy with the arrangement as she kept telling me that she hardly ever saw me – that I came home in the dark and left again in the dark, but I kept reminding her that it was only for a couple of months.

The Hawaiian Pavilion was built to represent the Islands of Hawaii and the roof had five domes about thirty feet high that represented the volcanic mountains that created the islands. These domes soared into the sky and were supported by compressed air that filled them up like balloons and of course, if the air compressors failed, the mountains collapsed. If ever there was an electrical failure, the volcanoes would disappear in a great big hurry. As a backup, a natural gas generator would kick in immediately and keep the mountains and volcanoes filled. If the roof covering fell over the crowded restaurant, there could be mass panic and injuries.

One evening after I got there, the heavens opened and the rain came down in buckets. Suddenly a small bulge appeared in the roof; which was created by the weight of the water collecting at the low point of the roof. As the rain continued pouring down, the bulge continued to get larger.

The restaurant manager came running over to my office in a panic and asked me to come over with him right away. The tables were all set for dinner and he was afraid the whole roof was going to collapse. Of course, my first reaction to this was, "What do you expect me to do about it?" His reply was, "I don't know but please, please, come and see what you think." I went along with him and when we got to the restaurant, people were already coming in for dinner and I looked up at the roof and said to him, "Oh my God, this is a disaster."

The roof had a huge belly in it that looked like a giant swimming pool. How it hadn't collapsed was a miracle. If it did, it would kill anyone that was under it. I let a scream out and yelled, "Everybody, and I mean everybody get out of here now." I grabbed the manager and told him to get me the largest knife they had in the kitchen and the longest broom and some string quickly. "Then get everyone out of here." He asked me what I was going to do but I really didn't know at that point. I asked him to hurry and get me what I asked for and said that there was no time for talking.

He ran into the kitchen and in a minute he was back with a knife, a broom and some string. I chased him out of the restaurant and I tied the knife to the end of the broom and while doing that, I thought to myself that this might cost me my career but if I don't do it, the whole roof is going to collapse and may kill people.

I looked up at the canvas roof and looked for a seam in the middle of the belly and with one swipe cut a huge gash in the middle of the belly. The water came down in such force that it almost threw me against the wall; dishes, chairs, glasses, silverware, white napkins went flying all over the place. It was the last I ever heard about it again.

The Florida Pavilion was nearby and the engineer that was assigned to it was a very elderly gentleman. He was retired but decided to come to work at the Fair and he used to come visit me and would bring bags of Florida oranges from his building. Sometimes he would be sitting in my office while the girls were changing shifts. They didn't mind him being there either; as they would come and change their clothes and be walking around half naked. This old geyser just sat there with his eyes popping out of his head. He would reach in his pocket for his handkerchief and wipe the sweat from his forehead. Then he would get up and say, "It's time for me to leave, I can't take this anymore."

He would ask me how I could stay there and watch all those gorgeous girls walking around like this. Of course, he would be back the very next day. By then I guess he had cooled down a bit. At least the oranges were good and fresh. I got such a kick out of him but always worried that he would have a heart attack.

This was my first year at the Fair and I only visited a few pavilions – Florida, and G.E. I just wasn't interested. It wasn't that I had to stand in the long lines to get in because all I would have had to do was ask for the engineer and he would take me right in and show me around. Probably the long hours were wearing me down. I usually only visited them when Maureen came out to the Fair.

The Fair closed down for the winter in Oct. and it was nice to get back to normality for six months.

CHAPTER 15

We moved from Crotona Park that Nov. because our baby was due in Feb. and our apartment was too small. A friend of Gerrie's, Kay Clinton, grew up in a nice area near Parkchester and her mother got us an apartment at 1443 Taylor Avenue. It was a larger apartment – still one bedroom but enough room for a crib.

Gerrie and Anthony had a little girl, Maureen, that Sept. and Maureen was very happy to be living near her sister and her new niece.

Jim was born on Feb. 12, 1965, and looked so much like me that whenever I went to the nursery they never asked which baby I was looking for, they immediately picked Jim up and brought him over to the window. He was a very good baby and was always a great sleeper which was a big help to us.

April came around and the Fair was opening again for the last year and Pat Ferguson asked me if I would cover for his brother, Jack, as he was going to Ireland for a month. It really didn't matter where I worked and Pat asked me to stop in the next day and see Jack as he would be flying out to Ireland that night. I knew Jack and he told me that he was at Traveler's Insurance and he would be working the eight am to four pm shift and then going to the airport after work. He thought it would be nice if Jack showed me the plant and gave me a rundown on the operation.

The next day after work I arrived at Traveler's and Jack was outside the building waiting for me. He said, "Let's go over and have a beer at the Rheingold Pavilion and then we'll come back and I'll show you around." Rheingold Brewery had a huge bar and Jack and I sat on two bar stools and had a beer and we were still there when they closed and that was my introduction to Traveler's. I have no idea of how he got to the airport but I know one thing, he was feeling no pain. I was fine.

The next evening I arrived at Traveler's and I didn't know where to find the engineer. Obviously I did find him because I worked there until Jack came back from Ireland and had no problems. Pat sent me to the main entrance building. This was the building that housed the Fair's Headquarters – mostly offices, police department, fire department, etc. There were rows and rows of offices with names and titles on gold plaques and nobody ever entered most of them. The people whose names were there were never seen so there was nothing very exciting going on there.

The boiler room was so hot that you could barely breathe when you were in it. It was windowless and had no air conditioning – it was horrible. One day I went to work and opened the boiler room door to check the boilers and was hit with a blast of cool air. I couldn't believe the difference in temperature and there was an almost brand new air conditioner humming away. I inquired as to where this appeared from and all I was told was "Don't ask any questions."

On the other side of the wall from the boiler room was Police Headquarters. After the Fair ended, the Daily News had an article about all the theft that occurred during the Fair and they said that it was so bad that an air conditioner that cooled police headquarters had disappeared and nobody was ever able to locate it. I think they should have looked on the other side of the wall. If they did, they just might have found it...

There was a time keeper at the Fair whose job was to visit each pavilion and to pick up the time cards from the employees and bring them over to payroll. We became friends. He would come over and pick me up and we would travel all over the fair in one of those open electric wagons. It was fun – especially when you were on the payroll at that time. He was about 6'1" and weighed about two hundred pounds and I learned sometime later that he had a sex change – he was married and had two little girls.

I was leaving work one night and walked out with another guy who was leaving and he told me that he got his paycheck and it was the wrong check – it was for the wrong amount and had the wrong social security number. As we were walking along, I said to him, "Don't feel too bad as the same thing happened to me – the check I got wasn't mine either." He said the strange thing is, they have my name M. J. Donoghue correct but that's all. I asked him to repeat his name and he told me again and I told him that was my name also. We just exchanged checks with each other, he was Michael Joseph Donoghue. Now what are the odds of such a thing happening? We became good friends – he was a New York City Fireman that got his Refrigeration License and was working at the Fair as a second job. I guess you can understand how things got mixed up since they had two M. J. Donoghues working at the same job for the same company.

The second year was so quiet it was actually boring. Nothing ever happened at the Fair's Headquarters during the second year. I visited a lot of the other pavilions. Maureen would come out with baby Jim and meet me and we got to see a lot of the pavilions before the Fair closed. In Oct. of 1965 the Fair closed for good and I was back to my two jobs in Jamaica. It took me awhile to get used to working only eight hours a day but it was good to get back to a normal life.

A few weeks after the Fair closed, Maureen and I decided we should take a trip to Ireland to visit mom and of course, introduce her to her new grandson.

We had some business to take care of with Mr. Sweeney, the lawyer in Roscommon. I called him from New York before we left and made an appointment. We arrived in Knockcroghery. It was great to see mom, Chris and Eamon. Kevin had died a few months before in a car accident. The village had changed a lot. I was shocked at the number of people that had died since I was last there. The weather was cold, wet and miserable; late Oct. is not a good time to be in Ireland. The dampness was so bad that the wallpaper was peeling off the bedroom walls and Jim, who was eight months old, made every effort to help it along.

The first night we went to bed, Maureen climbed into bed then let out a yell and jumped back out again. I asked her what was the matter and she said the bed was so hot you could die. In Ireland they put the electric blanket under the sheet and you sleep on top of it. This one had been on for a long time to make sure we didn't feel the cold...

We were scheduled to go see Mr. Sweeney and realized that Chris was busy in the shop and Eamon was up on the farm. There was nobody to leave Jim with. I really wanted Maureen to come with us so mom said that was no problem. She called up the local school and asked the principal to send someone down to baby sit for Jim. Sure enough a short time later a girl of about eleven arrived and was wonderful with Jim. They picked someone that had a young brother about his age so they knew the babysitter would be capable. Can you imagine doing that in New York?

At the appointed time we went to Roscommon to see the lawyer, only to be told that Mr. Sweeney was not available today. I was really furious and told the receptionist that I had made this appointment before I left New York and now I am told he is not available and nobody had the courtesy to pick up a phone and call our house and tell us. I could not imagine that they could run a business this way. We were leaving Ireland in a few days. Our family had known Mr. Sweeney forever and he was our family lawyer as far back as I can remember.

As I was ranting and raving, a gentleman walked out from an inner office and said, "Excuse me – what is the problem? Maybe I can help." He introduced himself as Mr. Sweeney's son. I told him what had happened and he suggested we sit down for a few minutes and he would see what he could do.

He left and a few minutes later we were told that Mr. Sweeney was now available to see us. We were escorted to his office and he was sitting at his desk. He shook hands with us and said he was really sorry for what happened but this is what caused the problem. He said, "The town of Roscommon sold a tract of land to the Belgium government and they are going to build a factory that is going to manufacture batteries. They will employ six hundred local people and it turned out that the town doesn't own the property that they sold. The Belgium government gave them until sundown that day to get clear title to the property or the whole deal was over. This town definitely needed the employment and they hired him as their solicitor, so that is why he was not available.

Some years later when I was back in Ireland I saw Mr. Sweeney and I asked him whatever happened to that situation with the Belgium government. He said that the deal did go through and the factory was built and went into operation for a time. They then closed it and left the country.

We visited Maureen's relatives and my relatives and did a lot of driving around the countryside. I showed Maureen my old grammar school, which was now a stable. We visited the farm in Coolaphubble and I showed her where I had worked and slaved and lost my childhood. The area is now used for grazing livestock. No more plowing, planting, reaping. No more horses or wagons and no more war. I saw some of the equipment that I had operated now thrown rusting in the ditches. It brought back so many memories that I didn't want to remember and I hope that never again should anyone have to experience such horror and misery.

We visited Maureen's Aunt Lil and Uncles Tom, JJ and Ed in County Leix. We visited where my grandmother lived in Dysart which is about two miles from nowhere and had dinner with my Uncle Tom and Aunt Helen in Gailey. We stopped off at Gailey Castle on the River Shannon where I used to go swimming as a kid and of course, we spent time at the Bon Bon Café in Athlone, and we can't forget all the trips to look for Waterford Crystal.

Maureen really wanted to buy some Waterford and it was very scarce in Ireland. I asked why and they told us that they exported most of it to the United States and the dealers in Ireland had been shortchanged, which made them very unhappy. Of course, Maureen was able to find enough glasses to give us a nice start to her collection. We didn't travel too much as Jim was only eight months old and that kept us pretty close to home.

We flew out of Shannon to New York on Nov. 9th and were approaching Kennedy when the pilot was advised that the airport was in darkness and to re-route to Boston for landing. As we were getting near Boston he was told that he couldn't land there and to head for Providence, Rhode Island. As we approached every airport up the East Coast, he was told that no landing was possible. The crew had no idea what the problem was. The whole eastern seaboard was in darkness and eventually we were able to land in Montreal, Canada but still nobody knew what was happening.

We stepped off of the plane into the crisp, clear Canadian air – the stars were sparkling in the sky and you felt like you could reach up and touch them. It was some change from Ireland's cold, dreary, misty, damp weather. The captain announced that we would be spending the night in Montreal and we would be transported to a hotel and hopefully fly back to New York the next day.

We were informed that all of our belongings had to be removed from the plane as this plane had to leave Montreal to make room for other planes to land and our flight tomorrow would be on a different plane. The airport in Montreal had a corridor that was nine tenths of a mile long and we had to carry Jim and the diaper bag, blankets, and all the boxes of Waterford Crystal, which were all part of our carry-on luggage.

We were bused to a beautiful hotel. When we arrived there was a crib for the baby and we were able to have dinner which was being served in the dining room. Jim was served a complete dinner and they made sure he had plenty of milk for his bottle. Nobody knew what had happened and when we got back to our room, we turned on the television but the stations were all in French.

It was many hours later when we found out that there was an electrical power failure that knocked out the entire East Coast. The next morning, we were bused back to the airport and had to take that big trip back on the corridor. In those days, you had to walk out on the tarmac and climb up the stairs to board the plane.

We eventually arrived back at Kennedy. My brother John covered my job while we were away and he and my brother-in-law Anthony were trying to get to the airport to pick us up but got caught in the blackout and were tied up in traffic for hours. They had no idea where we were and somehow they eventually found their way back home in the Bronx.

John had done a great job at County Fair and everything ran smoothly. I went across the street to see how things were going there and my friend, Jim McKillop, told me that he was leaving this job and going to a new job. He wasn't sure how long the company would remain in business. He said that he had been there too long and it was time for a change. I asked him where he was going and he told me that a friend of his was a Custodian Engineer at the Board of Education and he offered him a job as the Engineer in his school and he said he was going to accept it.

I asked him who was going to replace him as I knew I couldn't because I didn't have a High Pressure Steam License. He told me they were going to get an Engineer from Local 30 – he didn't have a Refrigeration License either so they wanted me to continue doing my job there. I told him that if they wanted me to do that I would be happy to continue and he said that they specifically asked him to see if I would stay so I said, "Yes, I would."

I was so sorry to see Jim leave and I knew I would really miss him. When he left, his replacement was Bill, a German fellow. He told me that he had been in the

German Army during World War II. He had been drafted shortly before the war ended and was never in combat. He said the closest he had gotten to combat was when his unit was on a hillside and a convoy of U.S. Army trucks passed beneath them on a highway. "We were very happy that they never saw us." He was a nice guy and we would sit and talk about all kinds of things. He was married and had children but that's all I knew about his personal life.

He worked there for three or four years and one day the owner of the company called me and asked me to come over right away as he needed to see me. I went right over to see what was so important and when I got there, he told me that the police were down in the boiler room and they were going to arrest Bill. He had told the police that they couldn't take him from the building until someone was there to cover his job as the plant had to have an engineer present at all times.

They called Local 30 and asked them to send someone immediately, but they didn't have anyone to send so they told them to call me and for me to cover the plant for now. I had no legal right to cover that plant as I didn't have a Stationary Engineer's License.

I still didn't know why Bill was being arrested. As I entered the boiler room and a policeman asked me, "Are you the replacement?" I said, "Yes" and they immediately cuffed him. I didn't get to even speak to him or to say goodbye.

Bill was charged with exposing himself to a young girl on Jamaica Avenue. The only news I ever got about him was the next day after his arrest, he suffered a heart attack and was in the hospital. I never heard from him or his family. Many years later I heard that he had died.

CHAPTER 16

In July of 1966, Maureen's cousins, Rosaleen and Ray Hoeymans, told us they were moving from the Bronx to Rockland County. They asked us to come up and look at the property where they were building their house in Spring Valley. During that week Maureen had been to the doctor and confirmed that she was pregnant and we now would have two babies in a one bedroom apartment. We knew it was time for us to start looking at houses too.

Maureen's brother Ed and his family had moved to Nanuet – also in Rockland County. We asked Ed to start looking at houses for us. We spent several weekends house hunting. One day Ed called and said, "I found the house for you." That weekend we went up to New City and bought our house at 57 Oak Road. We moved in at the end of Aug. – two days after Rosaleen and Ray. It was a great feeling to have some of the family nearby.

Commuting to Jamaica, Queens from New City made my day a lot longer. Gerrie and Anthony, John and Kathleen and Mary and Neil McCarthy all bought houses in New City that year, which made it really nice.

We woke up on Christmas morning in 1966 to the snowstorm of all snowstorms. It took me five hours to clear the driveway so we could go down to the Bronx to Maureen's parents' for dinner. It was really nice for all the family to be together and Jim and Maureen Garvey had a great day with all the gifts they received.

During dinner we brought up the subject of moving Christmas dinner to New City in the future. Maureen's mom had been hosting that holiday since they were married and now that we all lived in Rockland it made more sense for them to come up to us than for all of us to go down there. From that day on, we have hosted Christmas dinner and continue to do so to this day.

Maura was born on Feb. 3, 1967, in Good Samaritan Hospital in Suffern. She came home three days later during one of the biggest blizzards that hit our area in years. I don't think we were able to get out of the house for days – it was unbelievable. Jim was thrilled to have a new sister but was more interested in playing out in the snow.

Maureen said that when I came to see her in the hospital after the baby was born, my color was as green as the scrubs they gave me to wear. I was dying with stomach pain at that time and the next day I ended up at the doctor. I was diagnosed with an ulcer. I suffered unbelievably with them every spring and fall. The doctor told me to stop smoking, but I never listened to him. It took me until 1980 to quit. For the past 29 years I never had another cigarette or an ulcer attack --if only I had listened to the doctor sooner.

In the spring of 1968 we decided we should get a dog for the children. We decided on a poodle and the children called him Peanuts. He was truly Maura's dog. Maura didn't walk until she was 15 months old and she would crawl around the floor and Peanuts would be right at her feet. Sometimes he would have a hold of the back of her pants and she would drag him around the house.

One night after dinner, Peanuts was chewing on a steak bone. We looked over and Maura was on one end of the bone and Peanuts on the other. So much for all that sterilizing Maureen was doing.

Years later when she started kindergarten she would walk to Link School with Jim. kindergarten was only a half day and you would always know when Maura was on her way home – Peanuts would bark and bark until you let him out so he could go down the street to meet her. He and Jim spent hours playing ball together but there was no question Maura was his favorite and she idolized him.

That Oct., my sister Anita got married to Eamonn Martin and mom came over from Ireland for the wedding. Kathleen and John lived across the street from us and my sister Maureen and her husband Bill lived in Washington Township, New Jersey. Mom could not get over the beauty of the suburbs of New York City. She told us one evening that had she known there were places like Rockland and Bergen Counties when she was living here, she would never have returned to Ireland. How different our life might have been. Maura and Jim loved having Nana D living with us and missed her terribly when she left.

Maureen's mom died suddenly in March of 1969 of a heart attack at the age of 62. This was a great shock to all of us as she had never been sick. I missed her terribly – she truly was a second mother to me and to this day I feel like I lost one of my best friends. She was the best mother-in-law in the world.

By then I had completed my five year requirement necessary to take the Stationary Engineers' Exam. I had been going to school and studying for the test. I took the written and passed. The practical test was given at Fordham Hospital on Fordham Road in the Bronx and I passed that so now I had my Stationary License.

I was still covering the two jobs and Jim McKillop told me that he was going to take the Custodian Engineer's test. He said it was a very good job and he hoped he could pass the test. He took the test and passed it and was appointed to a school in Queens not far from where he lived. He said his only regret was that he hadn't done this years earlier and he thought the job was the greatest. He suggested that

I take the test since I had my Stationary Engineer's License. I told him that maybe I would, one of those days, but I really wasn't that interested. I was doing OK where I was and was very happy.

Jim was a great friend of Johnny Andrea. Johnny was the head of the New York City Boiler Division and he liked to hang out at a bar on Jamaica Avenue. Sometimes he would call me and I would walk over and meet both of them there. They would both get on my case about the Custodian Engineer's test and eventually they talked me into taking the test. I passed and was appointed to a school in Manhattan – PS 145 on 105th Street and Amsterdam Avenue.

I left County Fair on May 16, 1970, and that evening Maureen went into labor and Mike was born that night. Maureen's sister, Gerrie, had given birth that morning to a little girl, Kathie, so the two of them were roommates at Good Samaritan Hospital in Suffern.

I had two weeks vacation before starting with the schools and I spent that time air conditioning our house. Some of the refrigeration contractors that were working in County Fair offered me all kinds of parts and pieces and when I put them all together I air conditioned our house – it was all second hand equipment but it was in working order. We used the air conditioning system for the first time the day Mike was christened and it continued to work for thirty five years without ever being charged again.

I started with the Board of Education on June 1st and it really was a great job – pay wise, benefit wise, etc. but I really didn't like it because I wasn't a person to sit behind a desk and push paper from one place to another. I didn't enjoy giving orders to people that were working for me and being held responsible for their mistakes.

I considered myself a mechanic. I got my enjoyment from planning, designing, repairing, etc. I will never understand how I survived the first year, but I did somehow. After a year, I transferred to another school – PS 75 on 96th Street and West End Avenue. I liked that school much better. The employees were much more intelligent – they knew what they were doing and they made life much easier. I spent 13 years in that same building and during that time I made a lot of very good friends, including Malachy and Frank McCourt.

Frank wrote Angela's Ashes, which won a Pulitzer Prize. Malachy wrote a book, A Monk Swimming. He was also a talk show host on WMCA and was fired from that job when he told a lady caller on his show – "to kiss his royal Irish ass". They came from County Limerick in Ireland. I went for a walk one day at lunchtime and on the way back, I was standing on the corner of 93rd Street and West End Avenue and Malachy was standing on the opposite corner. When he saw me, he called across the street, "Malachy, what are the odds of three Malachy's standing on the corner of 93rd Street at the same time?" I said, "I have no idea but I would say it would be one in a million" and he said, "Well there are three of us here right now." I don't remember the other Malachy's last name but we were all there at the same time.

Malachy was an actor and did a lot of commercials. There was a part for an Irish Priest and he got it and he told me that when you put that Roman Collar on, you have no idea how popular you become – especially with the ladies. They considered you harmless. He spent a lot of time in my office and I really enjoyed him – he had a wonderful sense of humor but was a real radical. I didn't like either of their books.

During the winter of 1970, we decided to add a family room to our house. We had to go for a variance before the town board, which literally took months and eventually we got a permit. I drew up the plans and we hired a contractor to build the room and another one to install the granite fireplace. They worked together so well and our room was completed with no problems.

Maura loved Mr. Rick, who was the son of the contractor and he would take Maura to the dump with him in his pick-up truck every time he was going. She was three and thought she was the luckiest person to be able to go with Mr. Rick to see all the "birds".

Jim was in kindergarten at the time and they were having a party in school. Maureen was class mother and had to bring in all the supplies for the party. She brought Maura and Mike into the classroom and left them with the teacher while she went out to the car to get all the party goodies. The teacher took Mike around for all the children to see the baby while Maura played with the girls in the class.

When Maureen got back to the house and was putting Mike down for a nap, she noticed he was covered with a rash – it was chicken pox. She had exposed the entire class to chicken pox. A week later Maura woke up with them and she wouldn't come out of her room as she didn't want Mr. Rick to see her with a rash. She was crazy about him.

Mr. Pozar, the contractor, loved Mike. He called him Sluggo. When the walls went up in the room he would take Mike and his walker out to the new room and Mike would fly up and down the empty room while Mr. Pozar worked. They were a wonderful family and did very good work.

CHAPTER 17

In 1973, Maureen and I took our three children on a trip to Ireland to visit my mother and Chris and Eamon.

We landed at Shannon Airport early in the morning. Mom had said she would be sending someone to meet us and drive us to Knockcroghery. This guy comes over to us, all smiles, with a big "Welcome home – it is so good to see you." He immediately asked how John, Anita and Maureen were and I told them that they were fine and he kept on talking but I had no idea who he was. I thought that he would say something that would give me a clue. We picked up the luggage and put it in the car and still had no idea of who he was.

Maureen gave me a kick and whispers "Aren't you going to introduce me?" I whispered back, "I would have, if I knew who he was." He kept talking and the hole got deeper and deeper and still I had no clue. We stopped for breakfast and at this point I had no choice but to tell him that I had no idea who he was and I asked him, "Should I know you?"

He said that he couldn't believe that I didn't recognize him – he was Val Flanagan and he went to school with my brother, John. Well that explains it – he was a kid when I left Ireland. I did learn one thing from this experience and that was – don't pretend you know someone if you don't. I won't fall into that hole again,

The children had a wonderful time. Jim loved helping Aunt Chris in the store and especially in the bar where all the customers would make a fuss over him. Maura and Mike loved the grocery side of the store – that's where the candy and ice cream were and they always visited Aunt Chris there. They also loved going out on the farm with Uncle Eamon.

They had a donkey called Ned and Maura fell in love with him. I think it was a one-sided affair. Ned wasn't very interested, however, Maura really wanted to ride him. I put her up on his back and gave her the reins and explained to her that when you wanted him to go to this side or the other side, you pulled on that side of the reins and then he would turn in that direction. Well, at least that was the way it worked with horses but donkeys have their own mind as to where they want to go – not to where you want them to go.

I let go of the halter and Ned took off in a gallop with Maura on his back screaming. He knew exactly how to get her off his back by running under an evergreen tree with low branches. One of them caught Maura under her chin and flipped her right off his back and he kept right on running. That cooled the romance but I think she gained a lot of respect for him, but a little less love.

The weather was absolutely beautiful and the children had a great time. My cousin, Mickey Gately, owned a rowboat and I took all of them for a ride on the Shannon River. We took some fishing equipment with us but we didn't catch any fish. Still they loved it. My Aunt Kathleen was over in Ireland on vacation and it was great getting to spend some time with her.

I must move away from our trip for a moment to talk a little about Aunt Kathleen, who was my all time favorite aunt. I was forbidden to ever use the term "aunt". She was the youngest of my mom's family and there was only a few years difference in age between her and my sister, Maureen. We were warned by her that she was to be called Kathleen – not Aunt Kathleen – that made her feel old.

She was a nurse and had done her training in England and continued living in England after she graduated. When World War II began, she joined the Queen Alexanders, which were the nurses that manned the hospital ships of the Royal Navy. They picked up the severely wounded troops from the battle fields of Europe and returned them to the hospitals in England.

One day when their ship was coming back after picking up the wounded from the battlefield of North Africa where Rommel was defeated by the British, she was going through the charts and noticed one soldier's name, "Malachy".

This certainly wasn't a name you normally heard so she went to investigate and found a young native African that was severely wounded. Puzzled, she sat on the edge of his bunk and inquired how he was feeling. They talked for a few minutes and then she asked him how he got the name Malachy as it's not one you heard of very often.

He smiled and said, "I've only heard it once before. That was the name of an Irish Missionary Priest that came to our village in Nigeria. I was his first convert and when he baptized me, I asked that he give me his name." She asked him if he knew the priest's last name and he told her it was Fr. Malachy Gately. He was Kathleen's and my mom's brother. He had been ordained in Ireland in 1932 and went to Nigeria after ordination. Father Malachy remained in Africa (except for a few vacations back in Ireland) until his death at the age of 73 on Sept. 8, 1979.

Kathleen had travelled all over the world and came to the U.S in the mid 1950's. She was single and worked in New York Hospital for about a year and then moved to Florida. Soon after moving to Florida she married Jim Worden, who was an electrical engineer for a TV station. They had a beautiful home in West Palm

Beach with a swimming pool. One day Jim went swimming and came out of the pool soaking wet and went to plug in the TV set. He got electrocuted and died on the spot. Kathleen remained in Florida and died there in Feb., 2002.

We took the children to Coolaphubble, where the farm was. They simply loved the baby lambs. Jim remembers most the mud bath he got when the car got stuck in a hole and he was standing nearby. When I put my foot on the gas and the tires turned, it splattered him from head to foot. He still talks about it.

The children loved visiting the bog and we stacked up lots of turf for mom. Maura was very excited to bring back a sod of turf for "Show and Tell" in school. When she brought the sod of turf up to the teacher to show her – the teacher thanked Maura for bringing back a souvenir to her. There went Maura's sod of turf and she never got to use it for "Show and Tell" or keep it for herself.

Mom would listen to their stories for hours as she laughed and laughed. Then later on she would quietly ask me what they were talking about – she didn't know a thing they were saying as she couldn't understand their accents. It was funny to watch this day after day.

By the way, Val Flanagan was home from Canada on vacation with his wife, Ann. I had gone to school with Ann's older sister, Maura Kenney. Once again I have to deviate from here for a moment – we will get back to that trip in a little while.

A few years before I left Ireland, two other friends and I were planning to go to Australia. Paddy Kenny and McGuire (I can't remember his first name) were going to live in Australia. I don't remember what happened but McGuire did leave with his wife and two children. Paddy Kenny went to Canada and I went to the U.S.

Paddy joined the Northwest Mounted Police and married an English girl. Tragically she died in childbirth. Paddy left Canada with the baby and returned to Ireland and bought an old run down castle on the banks of the River Shannon and renovated it and turned it into a beautiful hotel. It was a very lovely location, about three miles north of the town of Athlone.

One night while we were in Knockcroghery, Val and his wife Ann and Joe Shanley, who I had gone to school with, and his wife and Maureen and I, decided we would go to the hotel for dinner. I knew that Paddy Kenny owned it but I hadn't seen him since our plans to go to Australia almost twenty years before.

When we arrived at the main entrance to the hotel, I asked them to stay in the background so if Paddy came to the door he wouldn't see everyone. I knocked on the door with one of those large door knockers. A maid, beautifully clad in her little white cap and black dress with white collar and cuffs answered. I asked if Mr. Kenny was in and mentioned that I would like to speak to him. She wanted to know who I was and I told her I would rather surprise him – just tell him a friend wants to speak to him. As he approached the door, I stepped back a bit out of the light so he couldn't get a good look at me. I spoke as he approached and asked, "Do you remember an old friend from way back?" I'm not sure he recognized me at first but when I said my name, he said, "Oh, my God – do I ever remember those days when we were young."

I told him there were a few people out here with me and he told me that the hotel was actually closed because he was having a party for his daughter and her mom's family from England -- but please come in and join us. I introduced Val and Ann and Val said, "My wife is also a Kenny and it turned out that they were related". Boy was it ever a great party.

I didn't know women could drink so much. They were drinking straight shots of Hennessy's Brandy. I asked Joe Shanley what the approximate cost of a shot would be, converting it from the old one pound note. He told me the cost of a shot would be twelve shillings and my immediate reply was, "Joe do you realize that when I left Ireland my mom paid a farm laborer twelve shillings a week with room and board? My God how things have changed."

We really had a very nice trip but the thing that would disturb me the most was when we went to Mass in the parish Church, there were so few people that I could recognize. It was embarrassing when someone would come over to me and say, "Welcome home. It is so good to see you", and I wouldn't know who they were. The real kick in the head was when someone asked me, "Where do you fit in – in the family?" Then I realized for the first time that this works both ways -- they don't know me and I don't know them.

After I had purchased the house and land from Fred Jackson, the contents of the house were auctioned off and mom attended the auction. She was interested in a beautiful French clock and the candelabras that were on the mantel over the fireplace in the sitting room. She really wanted that set.

At noontime, most of the people left for lunch and only a few remained at the auction. During that time the clock and the candelabras were put up. One person put in a bid on the candelabras – but not the set. Mom realized that the person who put the bid in was a nephew of the deceased Jackson ladies and she wouldn't bid against him. He got the candelabras and then the clock came up as a separate issue. Mom put up a bid of three pounds ten (less than ten American dollars) and no other bid was made and she got the clock. She could not believe that nobody bid against her but then she realized that practically everyone was out to lunch.

The clock was beautiful. It was bronze and stood about twenty inches tall – ten inches wide. It is late eighteenth century. Everyone in the family wanted the clock but mom told me she wanted me to have it, but she said there was one condition and that was that I had to come to Ireland to pick it up. Not only did I come to Ireland but the whole family came with me – Maureen, Jim, Maura and Mike.

Of course we hadn't given any thought as to how we would transport it – it was very heavy. I had to partially dismantle it and put all the parts into a large carry-on bag. Only then did we start to worry about the legality of bringing an antique into the U.S. We had no idea how Customs would look at this.

I just carried the bag on the plane and put it under the seat. When we arrived at Customs in New York, I didn't put that bag with the rest of the luggage hoping it would not be noticed. Considering there were five of us, we had a lot of luggage and when we got to the inspector, I stood in the background holding the bag with the clock.

The inspector looked at all the bags. He didn't open any of them but asked if we purchased anything at the Duty Free Shop. Maureen said "Yes", and opened her bag to take out the receipts and the next thing I heard him saying to Maureen, "Where did you get that wallet?"

Maureen got nervous and she said, "I bought this in the states before I left home." He said, "No, you don't understand, that is a replica of a very expensive wallet and I have not been able to find one anyplace. Could you give me the address of the store that you bought it in?" Maureen said, "Sure" and he gave her a pencil and paper to write down the name of the store and directions to it. He was very grateful and thanked her. Then he called over an employee and told him to help this family with their luggage out to their car.

All this time I did not know what all the talk was about – I was concentrating on keeping the children occupied and wondering about the clock. The perspiration was running down my face and the clock was getting heavier and heavier and I was thinking to myself, why doesn't Maureen just give him the wallet? Later Maureen said, "I would have but I never gave it a thought, my mind was on the clock." Later we learned that there are no restrictions on bringing antiques from Ireland to the United States. For once, "holding the bag" wasn't all that bad.

When we returned home, the clock found a home on the mantle in our family room, and keeps perfect time to this day. In Nyack, at an antique store, we found candelabras that went very well with the clock and they look as if they were made for each other.

CHAPTER 18

In Jan., 1974, Maureen started to work at P.S. 75 in Manhattan as my secretary two days a week. She would leave home after Jim and Maura went to Link School and she brought Mike with her and he attended the pre-kindergarten class at P.S. 75. He was so excited because he was now a "Big boy who was going to school like Jim and Maura." Every once in a while they would get diverted off the West Side Highway at 125th Street due to construction and that is where the meat market was and that was Mike's favorite place – he wanted to live there. He loved trucks. Even at that young age, he had high ideas....

That winter we drew up plans to install a deck on the back of the house and over Memorial Day weekend, I started laying out the deck. On Memorial Day, I started digging the footings and by evening I had completed digging and pouring twelve footings. Later that night I suffered a heart attack and was rushed to Nyack Hospital. The Cardiologist was very sympathetic – he asked me, "Why didn't you just climb into one of the holes and just have someone cover you with the dirt?" Maureen hired Mr. Pozar and Rick to complete the deck while I was in the hospital. She wanted to make sure I didn't go back to working on it when I got home.

Our neighbor's son, John Gritmon, was in college and used to work for me when he was on vacation. I would pick him up in the morning on my way to work and he would come down with me to the city and work in the school and make some money for tuition. That summer he ended up in the hospital with appendicitis so we both spent that summer recuperating on our deck.

John loved hearing stories about Ireland and he always said that one day he would get to Knockcroghery – he didn't know how or when but he would. About 30 years later John called me one night from outside our home in Knockcroghery – he was there and had a drink in our bar that we talked about many, many years ago.

One day our doorbell rang and when I opened the door, a young man was standing there and had a small Roman Collar on. I said hello, and he asked me if I was Malachy Donoghue and I told him that I was and he told me he was my cousin from Ireland. He told me that he was my Uncle Pat Gately's son – I can't remember his name. I asked him about the collar and he told me that he was an Irish Christian Brother. I said, "You know – I dislike you already" and he laughed and said, "I bet you had them in school" and I told him that I did. His answer to that was, "We are not like that any more." I added, "Well anything has to be an improvement."

He joined John and I on the new deck. The railing hadn't been installed yet but we sat outside and had something to eat and drink and then he left and we never saw or heard from him again. I don't know how long he stayed in New York.

The children often talked about our trip to Ireland but we noticed that none of them showed any interest in living there. To this day, Mike, who was only three at the time, remembers more about that trip than anyone – which always amazes us.

By this time, Jim developed an interest in scouting and when he got his Cub Scout uniform and first badge – he thought he was General McArthur – he was so proud of it. What we really weren't aware of was – when your son joins Scouts, so does mom and dad. Oh boy – were we involved and often asked ourselves, "When does this end?" Little did we know that Jim would stay in scouting through high school.

Life was busy at home. Maura was taking Irish Step Dancing lessons and joined girl scouts and 4H and was taking clarinet lessons at school. Maureen was totally involved in PTA and Mike went along for the ride wherever the others were going.

Shortly thereafter, Jim started to show an interest in Ham Radio and started studying Morse code, which is one of the many requirements you have to meet in order to get a license. The second major requirement is understanding the fundamentals of electricity, frequencies and aerials, etc. That is where I got involved. I was of some assistance in parts of it but Morse code was not one of them. However, by helping him, I developed an interest in it and before long, I thought to myself, why not try for a license with him?

We took the first test together and he received 99% on the code part. I just barely made it in under the wire. He didn't do as well on the theory and I got 90% on that part. When it was over, we both were licensed and this allowed us to go on the air using Morse code, which had limited power and limited frequencies. Our call letters were: WA2LLT and WA2LLV. Jim was one of the youngest licensed Hams.

We did have enough power to get ourselves in trouble with the FCC so we had to be very careful. The Ham Radio Operator, even with the first license, has enough power to transmit his signal to anywhere on the planet and the license dictates on what frequencies you can operate. You must be absolutely sure that you do not cross that line because if you do, you can be fined thousands of dollars and lose your license. If you accidentally cross into restricted frequencies, you could interfere with the launch of a spacecraft. Every transmission is monitored by the FCC to prevent this from happening.

At this time our house looked like it was going to be launched into space. Every tree in the back yard had an aerial on it and the roof had aerials of every size and shape. I divided our recreation room downstairs into a room we called "The Radio Shack" and that was where all our equipment was and where you would find Jim at all hours of the day and night.

Sometime later, Jim and I took our General License Exam. I was able to get my Morse code up to speed and passed the test and was issued the license N2AOH and Jim was issued the call letters N2AOG. This gave us the right to go on the air using either voice or code and gave us access to a broad range of frequencies. This time we added more aerials to the back lawn.

I rarely went on the air but Jim was in contact with people all over the world. He spoke to people in places I didn't even know existed. He had a room full of equipment and could be on the air using Morse code and be looking up places on a map or in the log book all at the same time. After contacting someone, Hams exchange post cards with their call letters on them and before long the walls of the shack were covered with post cards. Not only was it educational but it was a fabulous pastime for Jim and he really loved it.

Between Boy Scouts, Ham Radio and work, there really wasn't much time for anything else. On weekends the scouts had paper drives, trips to Camp Bullowa, lots of work working on merit badges and most memorable were the Klondike Derbies where we froze to death and spending a week at Ten Mile River Scout Camp as an Assistant Scout Master, helping out the Scout Master wherever I could.

We visited Jim at the National Scout Jamboree in Moraine State Park in Pennsylvania. The dads went along on camping trips to Gettysburg, Valley Forge, Boston, Philadelphia and Washington, DC.

When we went to Washington, DC I was responsible for a group of scouts. At one point we stopped at the Space Museum and I got so engrossed in everything there that the next thing I knew I was all alone and there wasn't a trace of a Boy Scout anywhere. There were crowds of people everywhere and not a red beret in sight. Eventually I gave up searching – went outside and saw a soda machine so I bought a can of Pepsi. I noticed an elevated wall and decided to sit up on top of it where I could view the surrounding crowds. I felt that eventually someone would come from someplace.

There was a sightseeing guide with a couple of people standing just below where I was sitting and he was pointing out all the points of interest to them, including the Ford Theatre where President Lincoln was shot, including the house he was taken to after he was shot and all the important places around. I had my own private guide, but still no Boy Scouts in sight.

Eventually, I saw a group of red berets coming up the street. They were safe and sound. Of course, I hollered at them for getting lost.... I was, however, able to give them a detailed history of the area and nobody thought to ask where I got all my information. They had a wonderful time in Washington, D.C.

Another most interesting trip was when we went to Gettysburg. The morning that we were scheduled to leave, I woke up with a fever. I was burning up. Of course, I couldn't disappoint Jim so I decided to go anyway. I remember arriving at a park by the Delaware Water Gap. It was freezing cold. We had brought bag lunches and sodas with us. While we were sitting on wooden park benches eating our lunch, the wind would cut right through you. Every time I cross that bridge, I still get tremors at the memory of our trip there.

We finally arrived at Gettysburg and we had to set up our tents in the dark. Just outside the battleground, we were camping and it was freezing cold. I got into my sleeping bag and did fall asleep and sometime during the night I woke up and was burning up from fever. I got up and got dressed and was walking around the battlefield in the dark and at that point my fever broke and by morning, I was just fine. While the boys were doing their ten mile hike around Gettysburg, Jim Furey, Chris Meenan and some of the other dads and myself took a ride into the town and found a local bar and stopped in there for a beer. We thought nobody would notice we were gone. However, at the next troop meeting, when the boys were given their patch and medal for doing the hike at Gettysburg, they called us up and gave us one half a badge and no medal. They realized we had left and found out where we had gone. We never heard the end of it. That story grew and grew all through the years we were involved in scouting.

Another trip that stands out in my mind was the one to Valley Forge. We did a ten mile hike in pouring rain. The only one of the boys that stayed dry was Dennis Riordan; the newest scout in the troop. His poncho was so big that it covered him from the top of his head to his boots. He made out the best of all. I will always remember one of the Assistant Scout Masters, Don Fairbanks. Don was always impeccably dressed and totally organized. Well, when he came off that trail, he looked like a drenched rat – it's a sight I will always remember.

Every winter we would go up to Camp Bullowa for the Klondike Derby. It always seemed to be on the coldest weekend of the winter. I remember sleeping out in a sleeping bag in the snow at five below zero. Luckily we had bought very good down sleeping bags so we were fine. We were outside all day Saturday while the boys raced their homemade sleds across the lake. Something that I'll always remember was the huge pots of chili that awaited us in the Rec Hall. Whoever made them should have gotten a gold medal – the chili was delicious.

The thing that puzzled me most was how those kids would suffer through some of those hikes and freezing weather and if the opportunity arose a week later, they

would do it all over again and love it. I was never able to understand them –
Scouts and Scoutmasters are a breed unto themselves.

The training that those boys received was amazing. It will remain with them
forever. I know the parents that went through it with them remember it also – that I
am sure of. The friends the boys made during those years also were some of their
closest friends outside of scouting and remain friends even to this day.

Maureen and I made some wonderful friends among the parents of those boys and
we continue to keep in touch with them. We still get Christmas cards from many of
the boys that Jim was in scouting with, even though they have moved away, gotten
married and have children. They were a great group. Maureen and I were very
proud of Jim – he hung in there and achieved the rank of Eagle Scout.

1974 was the year of the gas shortage. Maureen would fill up her car for me
because none of the gas stations were open when I left for work in the morning.
She and Mike would leave the house early in the day and spend hours on line
waiting to get gas. When I got home from work, I would siphon the gas out of her
car and transfer it into mine and she would repeat that whenever she was eligible
to get gas again.

Maureen would bring books to read to Mike and to this day he says that's where he
developed a love for reading. Maybe the gas shortage played a part in Mike
becoming an English teacher....

CHAPTER 19

In the summer of 1975 we went down to Manasquan, on the Jersey shore with Kay and Jack Garvey along with their children for a week's vacation. When we arrived it was pouring rain and we thought that this wasn't a good start to a vacation with six children in the house. Later the sun broke through so that made our start much better and remained that way for the rest of the week. We discovered that the vacant lot behind the house was now being used as an amusement park with a ferris wheel and all kinds of rides, music, noise, etc. The kids thought this was the greatest; the parents thought otherwise.

Jim and John Garvey couldn't wait to get on the rides and eventually I agreed to go with them. They were so excited – John was nine and Jim was ten and they wanted to go on every ride that was there. I suggested they go on one particular ride and it turned out to be a pretty wild one. It twisted and turned and spun in all directions and the speed picked up until it was flying. When they got off the ride the two of them were green. They could hardly stand up. John said he was going to throw up and Jim said he was sick also. The whole week went by and neither of them ever asked to go on that ride again.

When we weren't on the beach, we were fishing for red snapper and we caught quite a few. One night Kay and Maureen volunteered to cook them for dinner but we never got to eat them because while they were cooking, Eileen Garvey decided to jump over the fence with her fishing pole and jump to the ground. While she was doing that the line on the fishing pole flew around and the hook went right through her lip and we couldn't get it out. Kay and Jack spent the evening at the emergency room in the local hospital and when the snappers were cooked, we took a picture of them so they could see what they looked like before we threw them away.

Even though the week started out with pouring rain, the kids got sick on the rides and a trip to the E.R, we had a wonderful week together and even today, whenever I meet Eileen she brings up the fish hook. John and Jim don't talk about their experience at the amusement park but do talk of all the fun they had. Kevin and Mike were four and five years old and were very happy on the smaller rides and each of the children had a friend. Maura had Eileen and loved to vacation together. We spent several delightful vacations at the shore with the Garveys – they are very special friends.

That Sept., Mike started kindergarten so now all three were in Link together. Maureen was busier now working two full days a week, being class mother and on the Executive Board of the PTA. We both worked on the school fair and the famous Tire Playground. The Link parents joined together and built a playground out of tires of all sizes – from car tires to airplane tires. It turned out fabulous and the children enjoyed it for many years. My project was the dragon and Jim, Maura and Mike thought they owned that part of the playground for years to come.

In 1976, we took a vacation to the Thousand Islands in Canada. It's a beautiful area and the weather was gorgeous; warm and bright sunshine everyday. We took the boat ride around the islands, which took several hours and visited the abandoned castle which the children loved. We spent a couple of days in Gananqua and they loved jumping on the trampoline at the motel.

From there we went to Hamilton, Ontario to visit Ann and Val Flanagan. The last time we saw them was the time we met them in Ireland when Val picked us up at the airport and I didn't know who he was. We had kept in touch all through the years. Ann and Maureen were going to cook dinner but thought it would be nice to sit outside and have a drink first. They both liked a Tom Collins but Ann realized she didn't have any Tom Collins mix. Val said he would go to the store and get some and I went with him. We had planned to leave after dinner and head to Niagara Falls that night.

Val asked me if I had ever been to a Canadian Beer Garden. I said that I hadn't because I'm not really a beer drinker. He said that he wanted to take me there and we could get the girls their mix for their drinks after that. I thought that would be fine and off we went.

I never saw anything like this place. It was about as big as an average sized gym with the bar in the center. The smallest order you could place was six glasses or bottles of beer. If you went by yourself you would have to order six beers but if there were two or three of you, you could still order six. The waiters wore change makers on their belts like the bus drivers used to wear in New York years ago. Each table had room for twelve people. I have no idea how many tables were in the place. It was almost full and it seemed that everyone was a school teacher. It was summer vacation and they were all off and Val knew almost everyone there.

They kept coming over to say hello and Val would introduce me as his friend from New York and they would insist upon buying us a drink. Since each order was for six beers in a very short time there was no more room on the table for any glasses or bottles. We got there in the early afternoon and by midnight we had drank more beer than I had ever drank in my life. I didn't know if I could stand up. If my buddies from Alaska and the bartenders up there saw me now, they would have been shocked..

When we finally got to the parking lot, Val said to me, "You are going to have to drive home because the police keep a close eye on the people leaving here and I am drunk". I asked him what made him think that I was capable of driving since I didn't even know where I was and you think I can drive us home. He said, "If I get stopped they will throw the book at me but if you get caught you can cross the border and tell them to go to hell." I told him that I would not drive in this condition so either he had to drive or we could call a cab. He did drive and when we got back to his house everyone was in bed, lights out and stove off but there was a note in the kitchen that our dinner was in the oven.

Maureen and Ann thanked us the next morning for the Tom Collins mix that they never got. Maureen was ready to kill me because we were not supposed to be sleeping there, but it got so late they had no choice but to put the children to bed and to go to bed themselves.

We got ready to leave the next morning for Niagara Falls. Ann and Val suggested that we stay in a motel that they stayed in when they were there a short time before. They couldn't remember the name of the motel so they drove to Niagara Falls with us and found it, because they thought it was such a nice place for the children.

We had a lovely time in Niagara Falls and took the boat ride on the Maid of the Mist and the tour behind the Falls. The children loved getting all dressed up in the slickers and rain-hats and going under the Falls with the water pouring down on them. They still talk of that vacation as one of their favorites. Years later when Mike was in college in Syracuse, Maura came with us to see him and we drove up to Thousand Islands again and stopped at the same motel. They called Jim in California to say they were back on the trampoline that they had so much fun on years ago.

We also took a trip to Philadelphia that summer and each of the children had a favorite place that we visited. Jim was fascinated by the Mint – Maura loved Betsy Ross's house and Mike wanted to stay at the Liberty Bell. It was a very interesting trip and we got to visit Maureen's cousins the Rouleys whom we hadn't seen in a few years.

The school year was busy as usual and now with Jim in junior high and Mike in school full time the activities went on and on. The following summer we joined the West Nyack Swim Club and the children absolutely loved their time there. They all took swimming lessons. When Maureen went to pick Mike up after his first swimming lesson, he told her the instructor wanted to see her right away. She couldn't imagine what he could have done in forty five minutes that necessitated her being called in.

Maureen went down to the pool and the swim coach was waiting for her and asked if they could put Mike on the swim team. Maureen couldn't believe what the coach was talking about since Mike had just taken his first swimming lesson. He told her Mike was a "natural breaststroke swimmer" and he really belonged on their swim team in the under eight division.

From that day on Mike swam with the team and won many ribbons, medals and trophies and had some great years with them. He even came in second in the County Championships in the breaststroke one year so he had talent that we didn't recognize.

In 1977, we again vacationed with the Garveys and this time we went to Mystic Seaport in Connecticut. While we were at the pool that evening they announced that Elvis Presley had just died. Every year when Elvis's anniversary comes up, it is always talked about in the media and Jim and Mike will call home and ask if we remember where we were when Elvis died?

CHAPTER 20

In 1978, Maureen and I planned to take a trip to Ireland to see mom as she was getting up in years and it had been five years since we were there. We wanted to go during Easter vacation and when we tried to get five airline tickets for that week, we couldn't get them. The most they had available were three tickets so Maureen suggested that I take Jim and Maura to Ireland and she would take a trip to Arizona to see her cousins and take Mike with her and that is what we did.

This trip was planned around school vacation which was a total of ten days and we all left New City for Kennedy Airport together. Maureen and Mike headed west to Phoenix. Maura, Jim and I went east to Ireland and we met at Kennedy Airport ten days later.

One morning while we were in Ireland, I woke Jim and Maura up early and told them I had a surprise for them. I told them to get dressed quickly and we were going to take a train from Knockcroghery Station to Dublin. They jumped out of bed and were ready in no time. We left mom a note to say we were going to Dublin and might be gone for a few days. We left the house, walked up to the station and boarded the train for Dublin. After we arrived in Dublin, I asked them if they would like to see Paris. Of course they said they would love to so I found a travel agency and we bought three one-way tickets to Paris.

Later that afternoon we landed in Charles DeGaulle Airport in Paris and took a taxi into the city and went sightseeing for the rest of the afternoon. That evening we found a hotel and booked a room for the night. That was the first hotel I ever saw that the elevator went only to the eighth floor and then you had to climb the stairs to reach whatever floor you were on. There was a community bathroom on the floor, which was very common in Paris but foreign to us.

The next morning we were up very early and we went to the dining room for breakfast. The only other people in the dining room were a Japanese couple who were overjoyed to meet someone who could speak English to them. By the time breakfast was over, the husband seriously proposed that we switch children for their next vacation – their children would come to the U.S. and stay with us and then our children could go to Tokyo and visit them. He definitely caught me by surprise. I didn't think I was in a position to make such a drastic decision without Maureen. Afterwards I was sorry that I didn't get his address. We could have stayed in touch and I think it would have been a lovely idea for the children.

After breakfast we went on a bus tour which lasted several hours and saw quite a bit of Paris. In the afternoon we boarded a train from Paris to Calais and then we boarded the ferry that would take us from Calais to Dover in the southern part of England. I really wanted Maura and Jim to see the White Cliffs of Dover. There was a song during World War II that was very popular that went, "There will be blue birds over the White Cliffs of Dover tomorrow – you just wait and see".

The English Channel wasn't very cooperative; high winds and very rough seas. Immediately after we left the dock, I don't think we were more than five hundred feet from the dock, when the wind caught the ferry broadside. I was standing by the railing and suddenly the ship started moving sideways back towards the dock that we had just left and it picked up speed. When it slammed broadside into the dock, I really thought that the whole side of the ship would disintegrate.

What a start, but nothing seemed to be damaged. Jim sat in the enclosed area and spray was running down the windows. The bow would start to rise out of the water and the only thing that was visible was the sky, the fierce current caused the ferry to roll and bounce over the sea. It wasn't long before Jim started to turn green. He suddenly ran out of there and I really don't remember if he got sick or not.

Maura found a corner seat in the dining room and she curled up on the sofa. That's were she stayed for the whole trip. Hours later as we approached Dover, I woke her and said, "Maura look at the White Cliffs of Dover". She raised her head – looked over for a second and said, "They're nice" and plopped her head back down again and went back to sleep. So much for the trip, it truly was a wicked crossing. We then took a train up to London and later that evening went out to the airport to get a flight back to Ireland. As it got darker we noticed that there were very few people in the airport. What we didn't know at that time was that there was a labor dispute at the airport and most flights were cancelled.

I met a British Airways agent.   I explained to him that I had to get to Ireland because we would be flying out of Shannon two days from now for our return trip to New York. He said that he would love to be able to help but there wasn't a thing he could do as there wasn't a seat available.

His suggestion was that we take a train from London to Liverpool and catch a ferry from Liverpool to Dublin but the train ride is eight hours. Jim and Maura looked at me and said, "Please, dad, don't make us go on another ferry – we will die – please don't make us go."

Realizing our dilemma he then suggested, "Why don't you come back here very early tomorrow morning and go on stand-by for the one airline that is flying. Your chances are great that you will get a flight because the British don't like to get up early in the morning."

We left the terminal, got a room at the hotel and were back at the crack of dawn. We went on stand-by and were in Dublin having breakfast a few hours later. We took a train to Roscommon. That gave us time to pack up, bid our fond farewells and head to Shannon for our trip back home.

We met Maureen and Mike who had a wonderful time in Phoenix. They had gone to the Grand Canyon, which Mike loved and they got to spend time with all of Maureen's cousins. Mike couldn't wait to tell Maura and Jim about all the things the Easter Bunny left him in Phoenix. He saw his first $2 bill and was so excited about the five pound solid chocolate bunny that he received. Believe it or not, Mike received a solid chocolate bunny in the mail every Easter after that from Liz and Rich Jackson and that continued until he was in college.

Things got back to normal when we returned home – Mike made 1st Communion a few weeks later and could not believe that all the cousins in Arizona sent him Communion cards with several $2 bills in them. He still has those $2 bills in an envelope in our safe today.

CHAPTER 21

In June of 1980, Jim got his Eagle Scout Badge, which was a very exciting event and the ceremony was held in Link School auditorium. He received letters of congratulations, which were presented at the ceremony, from President Gerald Ford, Governor Hugh Carey, Senator Tom Morahan and all the local politicians. Several of our local politicians attended the ceremony and gave him beautiful plaques. There were over a hundred people in attendance and it was quite an event and quite an honor for Jim. He chose that date for his Court of Honor because it was Maureen's fortieth birthday.

During the summer of 1980, Maureen, Jim and I dismantled our kitchen and extended it by four feet. All the appliances and the sink were on the back wall which we removed and that meant that all the plumbing and electrical had to be removed and relocated. We removed all the kitchen cabinets and had to add twelve feet of radiation under the new kitchen window. We replaced the back wall with twelve feel of glass which gave the kitchen a completely new look.

We worked on it every weekend and it took us most of the summer to complete it. Maureen would say she never knew where the sink would be on a Monday morning – we were always moving it to a new location with a temporary hook up.

One morning before I went to work, Jim came into the kitchen – which was very unusual for him to be up so early, and while talking to me he was pouring himself a glass of orange juice. As he was doing this, I looked up just so see him falling backwards and the glass of juice went flying in the air and went all over him and he disappeared behind the sink and I heard his head hit the stove which was behind him.

I jumped out of the chair and found him out cold. I shook him and after a few seconds he opened his eyes and said, "That felt good." What he was referring to was the cold orange juice that spilled on him. He was burning up with fever. We didn't know it at that time but he had Mono. That really scared the heck out of me. He spent the summer recuperating.

In May of 1982, Mom died in Ireland at the age of 86. I didn't go over for the funeral because by the time I would have gotten there, the funeral would have been over. She had lived a very full life and fortunately her later years were relaxed and happy. She was a wonderful mother and I have many memories that I cherish.

Jim graduated from Clarkstown South in 1983 and left for the University of Hartford and so did the first of many checks. He studied Electronics for two years and at that point decided that he wanted to be a Chiropractor. After he finished in Hartford, he went to Los Angles College of Chiropractics where he received his degree. We had a lovely time in southern California after Jim received his bachelor's degree. Liz and Rick Jackson and Lil and Jim Mitchell joined us for graduation and we spent time visiting many places in southern California. This was our first time visiting this area and stayed in a beautiful hotel just outside Disneyland.

While we were there we planned a river trip on the Colorado River for the following summer with Liz and Rich, and Lil and Jim – Maureen's Arizona cousins. It was a three night; four day trip. Jim, Maura and Mike went with us. Each night we would camp out on the river bank. The guides would cook dinner and afterwards would take out their instruments. We would sit around the campfire and have a show or a sing-along. The next morning we would pack up our gear and put it back in the rafts and start our day.

I couldn't begin to describe the scenery – it was breathtaking. The previous winter there had been so much snow and rain that the river was at the highest level they had ever seen. In fact they weren't able to launch at the original spot. The raging river necessitated their selecting a calmer launching area.

The guides held a drill explaining what we should do in case we ran into trouble on the rapids. The most important thing to remember was to hold onto the safety rope that was connected to the raft. "Do not let go of it and you will come out of the rapids safely" but they emphasized, "Don't worry – nothing will happen – it never does, this is just a routine drill."

There were three rafts – the young people, including our three children, had the first two. They were usually in the lead and we followed. It was a fabulous trip and on the third day we passed through many rapids and some were quieter than others.

We hit one rapid that the other rafts had gone through but when we got there, we were hit by a wave that approached from the side and hit our raft and the raft shot straight up in the air. It flipped our raft upside down and landed that way in the middle of the rapid. All I remember is that I saw the wave coming and the next thing I knew we were airborne. Everything was happening so fast that I have no recollection of what happened after that.

The next thing I realized was that we were going through a rapid, the raft was upside down and I couldn't see over it but was still holding on to the safety rope.

The raft was three or four feet higher than my head so I didn't know where everyone was. All I could do was hold onto the rope. Eventually we got out of the rapid and the noise subsided. I still had no idea where anyone was.

After what seemed like a long time, my toe hit something under the raft and I thought – My God, that is a body under there. I know that nobody could be under the raft all that time and still be alive. I held onto the safety rope with one hand and I reached under as far as I could and I felt a life jacket, which I grabbed and pulled this body towards me. Then I had to push the body under the water to get it out from under the side of the raft and up pops Maureen's cousin Lil who was flipping mad at me because she was trapped in an air pocket under the raft and was doing very well in there until I grabbed her and pushed her under water.

I said to her, "Shut your mouth and try and get yourself up on top of the raft." I can't describe what was going on all around us. Maureen apparently got hit on the head with one of the oars and was knocked unconscious and floated down the Colorado River on her back. When the other raft was able to get to her and pull her out, she came to. Jim Mitchell suffered a mild heart attack but came through it OK and everyone else was fine.

We had most of the food supplies in our raft so there were watermelons, cans of soda and beer and all kinds of food floating by. I am sure the fish had a windfall and they could have recorded it but I don't think that all the cameras that went under would work under those conditions.

The young people were wishing that it had been their raft as they thought it would be lots of fun.. We went from there to Las Vegas – what a culture shock that was. It's very difficult to go from the beauty of Colorado to the confusion of a casino.

Aside from that one experience, it was a fabulous trip and the one that is talked about the most in our house. Maureen still says it was quite a 25th Anniversary trip—one she doesn't wish to repeat.

That fall Maureen and I flew down to Norfolk, Virginia to meet Bill Tracy. He picked us up at the airport in his lovely new Cadillac – which was a gift from Local 30 for his retirement the week before. Bill had been Business Manager of the Engineers Local for many years and he and Leah were moving to Florida but were stopping for a week in Nags Head, North Carolina for a vacation.

We were in the car about twenty minutes when Bill got pulled over by the State Police for speeding. He was actually clocked at ninety miles per hour and of course the policeman asked for his license and registration. When Bill opened his wallet to get them, the policeman noticed that Bill had a miniature police badge from the New York City Police Department pinned in his wallet. The policemen immediately asked Bill if he was "on the job" and Bill said that he just retired last week and the trooper handed him back his papers and told him to enjoy his retirement but slow down and stay alive. We reminded him of that lie many times when we would get together in the following years.

We stayed in their time share in Nags Head and one day we decided to take a ride to Cape Hatteras, the graveyard of the Atlantic. More ships have sunk there than anywhere else on the planet. We went there because someone had told us that the best clam chowder anywhere was made there in a particular restaurant. We were told it was well worth the two hour ride just for the clam chowder. At the restaurant we ordered the clam chowder and got talking to the waitress. She told us, "If you want to taste the best clam chowder anywhere – you should take a ride up to Nags Head. There is a restaurant there that makes the very best chowder you ever tasted." We enjoyed their clam chowder but we laughed because we drove from Nags Head to be told we should have stayed where we were. On the way back we visited where Wilber and Orville Wright made their first flight in Kitty Hawk, North Carolina.

We liked the Nags Head area very much and before we left we bought a time share on the beach. The next time we visited Nags Head was twenty three years later. We continued to trade time shares each year and we went to places that we probably never would have visited if it weren't for it.

One Saturday night that Oct. we were invited over to Gerrie and Anthony's for dinner and we walked in, with Maureen carrying a chocolate cream pie for desert, to be greeted by a loud "Surprise". All our family and friends were there for a 25th Anniversary party that we knew nothing about. Jim and Maureen Garvey had come home from college for the weekend, without us knowing, and it truly was a wonderful evening. We never figured out how they did this without a hint to us.

In June of 1985, Maura graduated from Clarkstown South and went to Marist College in Poughkeepsie. It was nice to be able to drive up and take her out for dinner and get to visit with her.

During those high school years we had five cars and I think I spent nearly every weekend under one of them fixing something. We were very fortunate that there were no tickets and no accidents, so we got through those years very well.

In 1987, Jim finished in the University of Hartford and that July left for Los Angeles College of Chiropractics. He and Maura drove to Phoenix, Arizona where they visited with Liz and Rich Jackson. They all went on to California and after spending a few days in Disney, Jim started school and Maura flew back to New York. Rich and Liz became Jim's West Coast parents during his years there.

In 1988, Mike graduated from Clarkstown South and went to LeMoyne College in Syracuse. We now had three of them in college at the same time. The house was rather quiet during the school year until they all arrived home for breaks. They all did very well in school.

Maura graduated in 1989 with a Bachelor's degree in Social Work and was named "Social Worker of the Year" by the college faculty and students. She went to Fordham University for her Master's degree in Social Work and was very fortunate to win a $20,000 scholarship from the union that Maureen was a member of.

Jim graduated from Los Angeles College of Chiropractics in Dec., 1990. Maureen, Maura and I flew out for the ceremony. Mike couldn't attend because he was having finals that week. As a surprise for Jim, Aunt Gerrie and Aunt Kathleen walked into the hotel room the night before graduation. Jim was absolutely thrilled that they came so far for his graduation.

After graduation, we spent a couple of days in southern California and one day we decided to take a trip across the border to Tijuana, Mexico. Maureen and I had been to Tijuana when Jim received his bachelor's at LACC but Jim thought the rest of the family should experience it.

We spent the day in Tijuana – Kathleen, Gerrie and Maura were in a state of shock when we first arrived but before long were purchasing pocketbooks, shirts, etc. and bargaining like old pros. Several friends asked us to bring back tequila from Mexico because it has the "worm" in it. When we were approaching the border patrol, we realized that we had two more bottles of liquor than we were allowed. Jim said he couldn't take a chance in being caught – he could lose his California Chiropractor License. They decided that Maureen could probably talk her way out of it but Maura would look the most innocent.

All the way to the border, Jim kept saying to Maura, "If they ask you how many bottles you have say ONE; then if they search you, pretend you forgot about the other bottle." He kept repeating "One" over and over and by then Maura was a nervous wreck.

As she stepped up to the Customs' Agent, he asked her, "Where were you born?" She was no nervous – she said "One." He said "OK – go through." Boy did we tease her about that one... Fifteen years later we still had some bottles of tequila in the liquor cabinet; I guess they weren't such a big hit after all.

Since graduation took place in mid Dec., we decided we would spend Christmas on the West Coast that year. We spent a week in Carlsbad, California with Kassie and Jim and then traveled up the coast to visit Kassie's family in Davis.

The weather turned extremely cold while we were in Carmel. It actually started sleeting. The meter-maid got off her bicycle and started running from store to store crying out, "Come out quick – it's snowing." This was very, very unusual for that area. It caused quite an uproar among all the natives. It wasn't snow but sleet, but a very exciting moment for people that never saw it before.

As we traveled further north, the farmers were running hoses and sprinklers so that the fruit would be encased in ice. It would be warmer inside the enclosure than out in the wind and cold. It was funny to see avocados, nuts, etc. surrounded in ice.

We had a lovely time in Davis and San Francisco – we visited Terry and Sharon Shauer (Kassie's dad and step-mother) and saw that their neighbors had gone away for the holidays and left their sprinkler system on. The ground was frozen so the water couldn't penetrate and stayed on top and became an ice skating rink. All the neighborhood children were on the lawn sliding around; some had skates and they were having a wonderful time. I can't imagine what the lawn looked like afterward.

We left San Francisco and drove to Phoenix and stayed with Maureen's cousins, Lil and Jim Mitchell. We spent Christmas with all the cousins at JoAnn and Ned Travers' house. Afterwards, Jim went off to the islands sailing with Rich and some of his friends before he started his first job as a Chiropractor. We returned to New York and had a second Christmas with the East Coast family.

CHAPTER 22

In May of 1991, Maureen and I went to Ireland. We rented a car in Shannon Airport and drove around leisurely. We stayed in Bed and Breakfasts and finally got to Roscommon as we had some family business to take care of. We stopped in Knockcroghery, my home village, and it was a very sad visit.

My family was all dead, the grocery store and bar had been sold and there was only one person in the village that I knew; or knew me. The only place that remained the same was the church that I used to be an altar boy in. The pastor was long gone. I didn't know who the present one was and I didn't know anyone in the area. I never want to experience that lonely feeling again. All I could say to Maureen was, "Please God let me get home to New York soon".

One of the nice things that happened in 1991 was that we paid off our mortgage and had a little mortgage burning party with our friends over. That was a great feeling. Jim had graduated, Maura had completed her master's degree and was working and Mike had only one year of college left.

In 1992, Mike graduated from Lemoyne College on his twenty second birthday. He spent the summer as a waiter in Lake George before starting teaching in IS 143 Eleanor Roosevelt Junior High School, in New York City that Sept. as an English teacher. What a great feeling; no more checks going off to colleges.

In Oct. of 1993, Maureen and her cousins organized a Ryan family reunion in the Poconos. Ryan was Maureen's mom's maiden name and they have many cousins across the country. It was a wonderful weekend with over a hundred cousins from New Hampshire to California gathering together. It's a time that will be talked about for years to come. Every time we get together someone has a story to tell about that great get together.

In 1995, we took a cruise to the Panama Canal with my sister and brother in law, Anita and Eamonn Martin. We boarded the ship in Acapulco, Mexico. While we were unpacking our bags and before the ship was getting ready to sail, Eamonn realized that he left all his shirts hanging behind the door back in New Jersey and had no shirts for the cruise.

He knew he had to buy some shirts quickly – we found a taxi driver on the dock and asked him if he could take us to a store to buy some men's shirts. He said, "I know the best place and you will get a very special price there because the owners are my cousins." This turned out to be one of the funniest but enjoyable experiences. He took us to some of the strangest places we had ever seen. They were like flea markets but you had to drive from one to the other. Everywhere we went, he introduced us to his uncles, aunts, and cousins.

He would drive into alleyways that were no wider than his car and they would open up to a maze of shops. Eamonn bought more shirts than he needed; we also bought jewelry, pocketbooks, t-shirts, beer and liquor. Anything you could think of was there. It seemed to be run by families; men and women selling their wares and children running around playing. I don't think many tourists knew about the market. They could never have found the place, or even know that such a place existed. He drove us back to the ship in plenty of time before sailing and we gave him a twenty dollar tip and you would think we gave him a hundred dollars. He hugged us all and invited us back to visit anytime.

We sailed down the pacific coast, past the Central American countries and into the Canal and sailed from west to east, which took eight hours to pass through the canal. We docked in Cartagena, Columbia in South America and went ashore. When we stepped off the gang-plank there were two lines of troops with machine guns and dogs. You had to pass through this line to exit the dock. It was a scary experience. When we reached the street, we got a cab to take us to the city. As we drove the highway, there would be a machine gun nest about every three hundred feet. The town was just about as warm a welcome as the pier. There were police and troops everywhere. They didn't deter Maureen from shopping; she knew Columbia was known for emeralds and she bought an emerald ring and earrings as souvenirs. We were very happy to get back to the ship.

Our next stop was Costa Rica, which was very nice. We took a bus tour of their capital city, San Jose, which was several hours distance from the docks.
The tour director wanted us to try Costa Rican coffee. He said it was the best in the world. Really it tasted like the coffee we always drank. Then he wanted us to taste their bananas. Again, he said they were better than any other banana, but we couldn't find any difference. At dinner he suggested we try the Costa Rican version of Baileys Irish Cream. That tasted very nice and we bought a bottle to bring home. When we did open the bottle at home a few months later – the liquid had solidified so we carried that bottle home for nothing. At least it didn't have a worm in it.

We also docked in St. Thomas, St. John and Puerto Rico on our way back and returned home from Puerto Rico. It was a wonderful trip.

In Aug. of 1995, I retired from the New York City Board of Education as Custodian Engineer from Brandeis High School in Manhattan. Maureen retired the same day but was asked to go back to work the following Thursday to help with payroll. She has continued to work one day a week ever since.

At this point our life changed from our daily routine of going to work every morning at six to days of rest and relaxation with time to travel. Life was very different from what it had been before. Then we were busy trying to earn a living, and now we were fortunate to be able to do and go wherever we please.

In Jan. of 1996, Maureen and I rented a very nice house in Phoenix, Arizona for two months. The house was backed up to Moon Valley Golf Course where the women's PGA finals are played. Neither of us plays golf but it was a beautiful location. Maureen has many, many cousins living in the area. Nearly every morning, Liz Jackson would arrive for coffee and after breakfast we would plan the day's agenda. Liz had spent most of her life in Phoenix, but she almost always managed to get us lost; not that it mattered, we had plenty of time and we did see a lot of the surrounding area.

We took a trip to the Four Corners where the four states; Arizona, Colorado, Utah and New Mexico meet and we sampled the fried bread that the local Indians baked. Every Friday night all the cousins would get together at some restaurant for pizza. Most evenings we would end up visiting one of the cousins or they would come to see us.

Rich Jackson loaned us a car. Jim and Kassie came to visit us from Sacramento and Maureen and I wanted to take them to see the Red Cliffs in Sedona. We heard that one of the nicest places to see them was an area called Snedley Road; very few cars used it because of its poor conditions. We had traveled it on previous occasions and we didn't consider the road to be in that condition. We had gone many miles when a rock punched a hole in the oil pan. It made a very loud noise so I got out to see what happened and there was crankcase oil all over the road. We waited for over an hour and eventually a car came by and took Maureen and Jim to a place where a phone was available so they could call for a tow truck. Kassie and I stayed with the car. Hours later the tow truck arrived with Maureen and Jim in it and towed us to Flagstaff. We rented a car and it took about a week to get the part because that model was so new, they didn't have replacement parts. Rich took the situation very well and invited us over to dinner when we called to tell him what happened. His reaction was; "Come on over and let's have a glass of wine and some dinner."

Maura flew out to visit and brought our dog, Shortie, with her on the plane. We visited the Painted Dessert and he sat up looking out the window – like he knew what he was looking at. We also visited the Petrified Forest. Maura met all the cousins and really enjoyed her trip.

We also had Rosaleen, Ray and Grace Ann Hoeymans come to visit, as well as Gerrie and Anthony Garvey and my sister Anita. We visited the Grand Canyon several times. It was a great two months and Debbi Crowley did a wonderful job in locating us an ideal house. We had a very enjoyable two months but it was still nice to return home.

One afternoon in the fall of 1996, Mike Garvey stopped in to visit. I was home alone and we were sitting at the kitchen table talking when he told me he would like to visit his sister, Kathie, in Peru. I said to him, "Why don't you? I will go along with you." He looked at me like I was crazy and he said, "You would go to Peru with me?" I said, "Sure, I think that would be a nice trip." Mike said, "Great, let's book a flight." I suggested we wait until Maureen got home, she might like to go with us.

A little later Maureen arrived home and we told her that we were going to visit Kathie in Peru and asked her if she would like to join us and she said that she would love to. A few minutes later, Maura walked in and the next thing we were booking four tickets to Lima.

We told Kathie that we were going but didn't tell her about her brother Mike – he was a surprise. A few weeks later, we were flying to Lima. Shortie, our dog, went to live with our son, Mike, who was living in the city. Shortie didn't like apartment life and let it be known by howling his head off constantly and almost got Mike evicted. Mike did say that walking the dog was a definite plus in New York City; every young female stopped to talk to him and the dog. Mike had a great time.

Kathie lived in a beautiful gated house with four other girls. They all taught at the same school. I don't know how they found room for all of us but they did and we were treated like royalty. The City of Lima is located between the Pacific Ocean and the Andes Mountains. The air is really polluted. The city is shrouded in smog and it doesn't clear up until about ten in the morning. The gasoline is all leaded and the air is foul. The traffic is chaotic; people riding buses are hanging out of doors and windows, bicycles are flying by and theft is out of control. If you put a piece of luggage down, they tell you to put your foot through the handle or else when you turn around it will be gone.

We took a bus from Lima to Pisco, which took several hours and then took a boat ride out to the Ballastan Islands. That was the first time we were ever close to penguins. They were so adorable.

Kathie and Warren Kelly, her friend, were great guides and their knowledge of Spanish was a great help. In Pisco, we were sitting in a restaurant and I was admiring a tree and I asked a worker if he knew what kind of a tree that was. He said, "Haven't you ever heard of a Pisco Sour?" I told him that I had never heard of it. He shouted over to the bartender, "Bring these people a Pisco Sour – they have never had one." He said that the drink was made from the sap of one of the trees we were sitting under. This delicious drink is very popular in that area.

The next day we took a six passenger plane ride and viewed the Nasca Lines, which were fascinating. The Nasca Lines are gigantic figures engraved on the desert surface representing fish, spiders and geometric figures, including an astronaut, which can only be seen from an altitude of no less than two thousand five hundred feet. There are numerous theories about their origins but no definite explanation; how they got there remains a mystery.

We flew over the Pan American Highway, which originates in Circle, Alaska, known there as the Alaskan Highway. This ends in Tierra Del Fuego in Argentina, which is 11,987 miles away. Little did we think at that time that we would be in Tierra Del Fuego a few years later.

We took a bus back to Lima and on the bus with us were a crew of workers that were returning to Lima. They were the rescue team that had worked pulling bodies out of the rubble following a major earthquake that had happened in the region.

The banks in Lima were so crowded that people had to stand in line for two or three hours to do their banking. They had to go to the bank to pay their gas, electric, telephone, mortgage and water bills. The lines were so long that people sent their servants to do their banking for them. Most exchanges of money were done on the street through money changers. You had to be very careful though because there was more counterfeit money in circulation than real money. Tourists especially were easy prey.

The best way to make the transaction was through a taxi driver. He would call a money exchanger over and tell him what he wanted. The driver would then examine the bills the exchanger gave him and then he would hand over our American money to the exchanger. He in turn would examine the dollars very carefully. When everybody finished examining each other's currency, the transaction would be finalized. We had a $20 bill that had a spot of red ink spilled on it and nobody would take it. There was nothing wrong with the bill, but everyone questioned it. When we came home from Peru, we still had the twenty dollar bill.

We flew from Lima to the city of Cusco on the east side of Peru. The flight took us over the Andes Mountains and took us from sea level to an altitude of 11,024 feet. When we got to our hotel, we were advised to lie down and rest awhile to get your body acclimated to the difference in altitude.

We did some sightseeing in the city and visited the Sacred Valley of the Incas and the Pisca Market. We spent the night at The Royal Inca Hotel and the next morning we boarded the train that would take us to Machu Pichu. This was a new experience in train travel. The train left the station going in one direction and then reversed in the opposite direction, then forward and backward again and kept repeating this while it climbed into the mountains. When it stopped, we were so high you could hardly see the city of Cusco – it was a little speck. The train had a crew on board with crowbars, picks and shovels. Their job was to clear the tracks when we had to stop because of rock slides on the mountain sides. Once the tracks were cleared of rocks, the train was able to continue its climb.

The train was often greeted by smiling, waving children when we passed through the villages near the tracks and when we stopped the men and women were selling their wares to all the tourists.

We crossed over the Urabamba River which thunders through on its way to meet the Amazon and we finally reached the last stop and boarded a bus which took us one thousand two hundred and fifty feet up the side of a mountain on a wet dirt road to the entrance of Machu Pichu. What a breathtaking sight in the clouds; you couldn't even attempt to describe its beauty.

This ancient city is among the best-known ruins of the world. Exploring Machu Pichu is not for the faint of heart. There are steps everywhere and steep drop-offs at every turn. The buildings are amazing and how all these rocks were transported there is the mystery of all time. Recently it was chosen as one of the Seven Wonders of the World and I can see why.

We returned to Cusco and spent the evening visiting a marketplace. Mike Garvey and Maura loved the jackets that they had on display and the people told them that they could order them. We told them we were leaving the next day and they said that was no problem. They would make them during the night and have them at the hotel by morning. They each ordered one and we ordered one for our Mike. The jackets were waiting for us at the desk in the lobby in the morning.

We spent that night at the same hotel. We had a large room shared by the four of us. During the night, I was kept awake by a dripping faucet so I called out to Mike to ask him if that dripping faucet was keeping him awake also and in the process woke him up from a deep sleep. He told me the next morning that he never did go back to sleep after I woke him up and in the future I should just keep my curiosity to myself. He still talks about the fun we had on this trip.

The next day we took a bus from Cusco to Puno, which was about a ten hour ride. Puno is the gateway to Lake Titicaca, which is the highest navigable lake in the world. It is one hundred twenty one miles long making it the largest lake in South America. Sixty percent of the lake is in Peru and forty percent is in Bolivia.

There are islands out on the lake that are made of reeds. They float on the water and families live on them. These islands are about seven miles off shore and the children use boats made from reeds to get to school. We took a ride on one of these boats.

Kathie arranged a wonderful tour guide for us and he took us out to one of those islands on a regular wooden boat, with an outboard motor on it. This is the thing that I remember most about this trip. When we got out about three miles, the motor started to sputter and then it just died. Well, the guy got all flustered as he couldn't get the engine to start. This was very serious as we could be out there for days and nobody would come by. He wasn't getting anywhere so I decided to give it a try.

Eventually I discovered that the cooling water intake was plugged up with seaweed. While I was up to my elbows trying to get this thing cleaned out, I look up and there is Mike Garvey stretched out on the back seat looking up at the sky and he said in a loud voice, "What the Hell are we doing here?" Of course, that really helped the situation. Eventually, we got the motor running and got out to the island.

Their homes were made of reeds, their boats were made of reeds and everything was supported on floating reeds. We took a ride on one of those reed boats and it was quite large. The Indian that took us out had to drag himself onto the boat and I asked him what happened to his foot and he told me that he accidentally blew away part of his foot with a shotgun. We told him to cut the trip short; he had enough problems, without entertaining us.

Mike Garvey did get an answer to his original question. He and all of us really enjoyed seeing how these people lived. The children sang and danced for us and were thrilled with the money we gave them and they treated us very nice. The women had numerous kinds of fish out drying in the sun – they were turning them over to dry the other side and were all sitting, crossed legged doing their work. That reminded me of the Alaskan ladies drying out their salmon on the river banks. Perhaps those we consider to be primitive have a better understanding of life than we do. We returned to Puno on the same boat without incident.

One interesting thing that happened was, before we left for Lake Titicaca, the guide had taken us to a shopping area where people were selling woolen items. Of course Maura bought several sweaters. Later when we were on the boat to take us to Lake Titicaca, Maureen went to take some pictures and discovered she left her 35 mm camera behind in the store where we had shopped earlier. We were very disappointed to have lost the camera and in the case was all the film to be developed of the pictures we had taken on this trip. This was before digital cameras.

That evening, when we returned to Puna, the guide suggested we go back to the store and see if the camera was still there. I thought he was crazy as we had heard so much about theft in Peru. When we got to the area where we shopped for sweaters, they came running out of the store; so happy to see us as they had our camera. They even stayed open during Siesta time that day in case we came back looking for it. We thought that was really very kind of them and of course, Maura bought more sweaters to thank them for being so nice.

The tour guide took us to his home before we returned to our hotel that evening and brought us some gifts as a remembrance of our trip to his country. This was the one area that the altitude really affected us all. When we watched the videos we took after we got home, we could hear ourselves actually gasping for breath – it was a horrible feeling. The next day we went to the airport to fly back to Lima.

We met a young fellow at the airport and we started talking and I asked him where he was going. He told me he was going to a town high up in the Andes called Arequipa. I asked him how long of a flight it was and he told me it would take twenty minutes. I asked him why he didn't drive there; he could be there while he was sitting in the airport waiting for the plane. He said, "By jet it is twenty minutes; by car it would take eight hours to drive; that is the reason I am waiting here, quite a difference in travel time."

We boarded the plane and twenty minutes later landed in Arequipa and discharged many passengers and then we flew on to Lima. Mike Garvey had such a great time that he called work and requested an extension on his vacation, which was granted, so a few days later we flew back home without him. It really was a wonderful trip and we were so happy that we went there.

CHAPTER 23

In Feb. of 1998 Jim and Kassie were married at the Sacramento Capital Club in California and what a wonderful turnout it was. The entire family; including our brothers, sisters, nieces, nephews, cousins and neighbors from New York, New Jersey, Virginia, Florida and Arizona all flew out a few days before the wedding. Rich and Liz Jackson had a hospitality suite where the family reunion continued despite the fact that El Nino was in town and it poured rain for days.

The wedding ceremony was beautiful and everyone partied until the wee hours of the morning. The following day we hosted a breakfast at the hotel before saying goodbye to everyone.

Rich Jackson was going skiing with the Garveys, Roussels and Hartigans up in northern California. Maureen and I were going to drive back to Arizona with Liz in their car. Rich had a GPS, which was very new at that time and he programmed it for the return trip home. We had no idea how to use it but he had it all set up before he left; that is until Liz turned on the car and started pushing buttons. She did such a good job that we couldn't get the GPS on and none of us had any idea of how to get where we were going.

Maureen got the idea to call Mercedes headquarters and ask for some help. The guy that answered the phone asked her which Mercedes she was driving and his comment to her was, "Rich but dumb." He said it in a joking way and she just laughed and he walked her through the steps to get the car and the GPS running.

We spent the first night in Carmel; didn't get very far that day and traveled to Palm Springs the second night. By the time we arrived in Palm Springs, both Liz and I were really sick. The next morning we were both so miserable and we had no idea what was wrong with us but later learned that the Hong Kong flu was raging in California. Maureen drove all the way to Scottsdale while Liz and I slept in the car.

We spent a week in Arizona and then flew home. As always, we had a wonderful visit with all the family out there.

On Aug. 5, 1999, Taylor Nicole Donoghue was born. Our first grandchild arrived. We were really thrilled but that word Grandpa made me feel old. She changed that to Poppy when she started to talk.

The following winter Maureen and I took a trip to Mazatlan, Mexico. We had some great times around the pool and every afternoon they would have a special "drink of the day". They always tasted delicious and when we tried to make them at home, they never were as good.

The song that was popular at that time in Mexico was "Follow the Leader, Leader, Leader". Every afternoon the staff would start singing this and have everyone following them all over the place. You never knew where you would end up. They were a great group.

When we made our reservations to go to Mazatlan, we were flying American Airlines and were told we would have to change airlines somewhere as American did not fly to Mazatlan. They asked if we wanted to go to Las Vegas, San Francisco or Los Angeles to connect with another flight. Maureen asked for San Francisco and said "Can you let us have a few hours layover as our family live near there and we could have them come and spend some time with us at the airport?"

The girl on the phone asked, "You only want to see your family for a few hours?" Maureen asked her how long of a layover she could have and she said you can stop for a week if you want and continue on with the same ticket so that was the first of many times we got to Sacramento while travelling somewhere else. Taylor had spent her first Christmas with us in New York with Kassie and Jim but it was very nice to get the opportunity to see them again a short time later.

We connected in San Francisco with Alaskan Airlines and there were only a few people on the flight so we sat next to two pilots who were going to Mazatlan to fly a plane back the next day. We talked the whole way there; they were very nice guys and we parted at the Mazatlan airport. The next day an Alaskan Airline plane crashed that left Mazatlan and was heading for Alaska. We never knew if it was the pilots that we had met were the ones flying that fatal flight.

In Jan. of 2001, Maureen's dad turned ninety five and we had a nice celebration for him. A few weeks later on Feb. 2nd, he died in his sleep. He was a wonderful guy and had spent a great deal of time at our house. We all miss him very much.

In May of 2001, our first grandson was born – Michael Christopher Donoghue. Maureen went out to Sacramento for a few weeks to give a hand at the house and the office. Taylor was only twenty one months old so Kassie had her hands full.

Later that year, we flew to Whistler in British Columbia, the most western province in Canada, and by far the most beautiful. Whistler is a very popular ski resort.

We were there on Sept. 11th, the day the Twin Towers were bombed and destroyed in New York City. I had just gotten up and was getting dressed and turned on the television when all of a sudden the pictures of the Twin Towers appeared. I woke Maureen up and said that I didn't know what was happening in New York but it appeared that the Twin Towers were on fire. Then it dawned on us what had happened. The announcer went on to describe that a jet plane had flown into the tower.

We sat and watched as the first one collapsed and moments later the second one. The city was in chaos. Security had taken immediate action and closed down all the entrances and exits to and from New York City. All bridges were secured and all entrances into the U.S. were secured and they tightened security on all points of entry. We knew that our children would not be in that area but our nephew Kevin worked there, and fortunately he was fine. We were sure we would know people that were hurt and killed. Maura and Mike had several friends that were in the Twin Towers when this occurred and sadly had died there.

Maureen and I were out of the country and driving a Canadian rental car and were about ninety miles north of the U.S. border. Everything remained closed and our hotel and car rental were up three days later. For days, they were announcing that the wait to cross the border was from five to ten hours.

I asked Maureen what she thought of the possibility of the rental car company allowing us to drive across to the states. No flights were being allowed into New York. Maybe we could drop the car off in Seattle, Washington and find our way to Sacramento.

Maureen said that car rental companies don't want you to drop off a car from one state to another so she couldn't imagine that they would let you do so from one country to another. I said, "What have we got to lose? All they can do is say no and we would be no worse off than we are now."

Maureen called and they said they would be very happy if we did that. They had so many Canadians in the U.S. that couldn't get home because of the situation. They were looking for cars to drive back. In fact, they told us they wouldn't even charge us a drop off charge if we would drive our car there.

On Sunday morning we left Whistler at four am and when we arrived at the border we had only a short delay. We dropped off the car at the airport in Seattle and eventually got a flight to Sacramento. We spent a few days visiting Kassie, Jim and the children before returning home when the airports opened up again.

In Feb. of 2002, we visited Cabo San Lucas, which is located on the southern tip of the Baja peninsula in Mexico. We had a condo on the first floor and a terrace on the front of the building overlooking the pool. Our suite was on the corner between two buildings and when we sat outside in the evenings, almost everyone going by would stop and talk. We met so many wonderful people from all over the U.S. and Canada.

It had only one problem. There was no swimming allowed in the ocean. It was absolutely forbidden. They said if you entered the water, there was an immediate drop of sixty feet of sheer rock cliffs. The plus side of that was that you could lie in bed and watch the whales that came by all day long. We were told that they come down from Alaska at certain times of the year. The attraction to that area was they were able to scratch themselves against the rock cliffs and rid themselves of all their barnacles. The creatures of nature always find a way. We have never seen so many whales in any one place.

Cruise ships passed by and you could almost shake hands with the passengers as they passed by. The pool was something else to watch. The older men in their seventies and eighties were wearing thongs and the young, gorgeous girls were flocking around them. What a waste.

One evening we were looking for a particular restaurant and we started walking and eventually we stopped a guy who was working on his boat and asked if he knew where this place was. He said, "Just look across the water and it is right there on the other side of the sound. You can walk there but you have to walk all the way around and it will take you at least an hour but I will take you there in my boat for three dollars."

We said that would be fine and we got into the boat with him. We were shocked at how rough the water was and when we got to the other side, he tried to get into shore but couldn't with the waves. He made several attempts but just couldn't get in. He really tried and felt very bad and apologized many times but said, "You are going to have to jump out of the boat and wade into shore." That's exactly what we had to do. The water was up to Maureen's waist at times but we made it and when we got there, we were soaking wet, but nobody on shore cared. The beach itself was one big drinking party. A maze of bars and restaurants were located right on the beach. We were dry from the warm breeze and eating shrimp in no time. I believe we ate shrimp every night that week. The freshly caught shrimp was a special treat. Surely in years to come the grandchildren will enjoy the saga of Nana wading to shore to a beach party.

On Sunday, we inquired if there was a Catholic church nearby. We were told that if we walked down the hill into town, just a few blocks and a few turns, we would be there. We did as we were told but no church appeared.

I stopped and asked a group of young guys if they could help us. They told us where it was and added; "Only tourists go there." So much for Holy Mexico. We eventually found it. It was a little building. No wonder we couldn't find it – we were looking for tall spires; not a tiny frame building.

We walked into the courtyard and all the windows in the church were open and there were as many people on the outside looking in as there was inside. Maureen and I sat outside on stone steps and the Mass was in Spanish and we didn't know one word they were saying. There didn't appear to be many tourists – if there were, they were all Spanish speaking.

On our way home, we stopped in Sacramento for a week and Jim and I built a shade structure for outside their house. Michael was then nine months old and crawling all over the place. Taylor, adorable at two and a half, was our helper. We had a wonderful visit with Jim, Kassie and the children.

In June of 2002, Mike and Robyn got married on the beach in the Hamptons. This special day was shared by all the family and many friends. It was a beautiful day and the wedding was truly wonderful. We always said that Mike never forgot an old friend, he just kept adding new ones and this day proved us right. Numerous classmates of his that started with him in Link School kindergarten were at his wedding, as well as friends from Felix Festa Junior High, Clarkstown South and LeMoyne College.

Everything went perfectly, except for the fact that Jim and Kassie's flight got delayed for twelve hours and their entire luggage was lost.

There was a major trip to the shopping center to get the four of them clothed for the rehearsal dinner and wedding. Since Jim was the best man, his tux was already ordered, but Kassie spent the morning of the wedding, assisted by all the Garvey girls, getting herself and the children clothing. Everyone looked great and yes, their luggage arrived at the hotel after the wedding.

CHAPTER 24

Life and time keep moving along. Unbelievable as it seemed, it had been forty five years since I was last in Alaska. In 2003, Maureen and I flew to Fairbanks and planned on spending a week traveling on our own. We had made arrangements to stay at a Bed and Breakfast. On the internet, Maureen had located one on Minnie Street, just a block from the house I had lived in and wrote her many letters from.

We located a car rental company and arranged to rent a car for a week. The problem was that the car rental company closed from twelve noon on Saturday and didn't reopen until Monday and we were arriving on Saturday afternoon. They asked where we were staying and they said, "That's no problem – we know exactly where the Bed and Breakfast is and we will deliver the car to their driveway on Saturday morning and put the keys under the floor mat." This way we wouldn't be without a car all weekend. That was very nice of them.

At the end of the week, we joined the Princess Cruise tour which was originating in Fairbanks. When we arrived from the airport, the car was there waiting for us.

After we got unpacked, we went into town, walked around for awhile and went to Mass at St. Joseph's Church; the only Catholic church in Fairbanks. It had gotten very shabby and could certainly use a good cleaning and a paint job. We sat up in the balcony, which was my favorite place to go to when I lived there. Then it was always crowded. Now it looked like nobody had been up there in years and there was only one other couple with a baby there. It was sad to see.

When we were leaving the church, the pastor was standing outside shaking hands with people. I said, "Father, this is the only church I have ever been to where the pastor told the congregation that he would not have any collection that day because he had more money than he knew what to do with." The priest said that he really wished that would happen today. Yes that was a long time ago – forty five years. Back then only silver dollars were circulated in Alaska; paper dollars were not in use. It was also a territory back then; not a state. The only other silver state in the U.S. was the state of Nevada.

It was still daylight out so we took a ride to the south side of town and stopped for dinner. When we returned to the car, the windshield had a huge crack in it that went down one side to about two inches from the bottom and then went all the way across. We were shocked and couldn't understand what happened. We hadn't noticed anything when we parked there an hour ago. How did we not notice it before? The whole thing didn't make any sense.

When we got back to the Bed and Breakfast, we told the lady that owned the house what had happened – or I should say we told her the story because we had no idea of what happened. She said, "Don't worry about it – I will call the rental company on Monday and it will be OK." She called that morning and they told her to assure us we shouldn't worry about it as practically every car in Fairbanks had a cracked windshield. Every spring they have to have them all repaired; unless the crack interferes with the driver's vision, then they would replace it immediately. This was caused by rocks flying out from under the wheels of passing cars. What a relief.

The Bed and Breakfast was owned by a husband and wife. It was a warm, friendly, immaculately clean home. There were three other couples and one single guy that were staying there. We found them to be the most interesting people. The only major problem was when breakfast was over, we had so much fun talking that nobody wanted to leave the table. We had to keep reminding ourselves that we didn't travel this distance to spend the day sitting around the dining room table talking. Luckily it was daylight until at least eleven pm so we had long days of daylight.

I asked Maureen if she remembered the address on Minnie Street that she used to write to me and she said, "Oh sure, it was 303 Minnie." Sunday morning after breakfast, I suggested that we walk down the street and see it. It was a very nice house when I was living there. After all those years, Maureen was able to feast her eyes on the house on Minnie Street where she had sent so many letters.

Actually, I spent one winter there while I was working for Northern Commercial Company. It was better than doing nothing. The winters there can be very long and dark and the temperatures can be anywhere from ten below zero to fifty-five below zero and can plunge in a matter of minutes from one extreme to another.

When we arrived at 303 Minnie St, it was sad to see that the house had gotten very shabby and uncared for. I told Maureen that I was going to ring the bell and maybe they would invite us in so we could see the inside. Someone came to the door and was trying to open it but apparently couldn't. It was a girl and she shouted out to us to come around to the back door, which we did. She was young and cute; definitely the flower child type. I introduced myself and told her that I had lived in the house over forty years ago. I knew she wasn't even born then. She invited us in to look around.

The upstairs was pretty much as I remembered it – but a mess. The downstairs was where I really wanted to see. That's where I had slept. This was a large area where we each had our own bed. Now it was divided into separate rooms and each door had a padlock on it so there wasn't anything to see.

That afternoon we went into town. This was a shock of all shocks. The old bridge that crossed over the Chena River had been replaced. First Avenue that ran along side the Chena River had practically disappeared. All that was left was the back side of two hotels and their parking lots and Second Avenue looked just as bad. Second Avenue was the heart of the city, both for day and night life.

The left side of the street in the fifties was all bars and the right side of the street contained all the stores that were of any interest. One of the most popular bars was the Snake Pit. You entered on Second Avenue and exited on First Avenue – I don't think they ever closed, day or night. You could hear country music blasting for blocks. This was the entertainment center of the city. There were very few women living in Alaska then. The females who were there were either Indian or Eskimo and were rarely sober. There were two movie theatres and one drug store. The drug store was the only one in town and was the place that people hung out in who weren't interested in bar life. The drug store wasn't there anymore. Sadly, the property was broken into a mess of little junk stores. The theatre remained but movies are no longer shown.

Northern Commercial Company was the largest store in town. They were the parent company of Hudson Bay and they provided all the equipment for all the trading outposts that were scattered across the remote regions of the arctic. They still were supplying prospectors and miners by bush plane.

When I worked for them I would watch supplies being packed in cardboard boxes and several bands of wire wrapped around them. The reason for this was there was no place to land a plane and supplies would be dropped from a low flying altitude. In remote regions, the only markings bush pilots have are creeks and rivers. There was nothing else to be seen. There was no contact with those people, so months before, the prospector had to tell the company what his particular location would be.

For instance, where a creek would meet a particular river they would make their drop. Those arrangements had to be made months and sometimes years in advance. When they came in from the bush, they settled their accounts. Today all traces of that huge company were gone. There was nothing in its place; I could not believe what had happened to it.

This place went from being a frontier town that was out of control to an absolutely dead town. We stopped into the jewelry store and I asked the jeweler what happened to the town.

He told me that when the Pipeline came through all the riff raff from the lower forty-eight came up looking for work. The Pipeline took two years to complete and when it ended, two-thirds of them returned to wherever they came from and the other one-third stayed. The crime got so bad that housewives were afraid to leave their homes and go into town to go shopping.

Some company got the idea of putting up a shopping center on the outskirts of Fairbanks and that was the beginning of businesses moving out to the suburbs and that is why the town was so dead. I thought the best thing they could do was dig a hole and bury it. That was the sad story of my visiting my favorite city. Even the railroad station had been relocated and the power house that supplied electricity to the region was moved also. I asked the lady that owned the Bed and Breakfast what happened to the railroad station and she asked me what was wrong with it. When I told her that it was not where it used to be, she didn't know what I was talking about – she thought maybe the road had been relocated.

The next morning, we drove down by the power house and then I knew why they had changed the tracks and the station. The power house was coal fired – the coal came in by railroad cars that had to be rerouted. The railroad tracks had to be moved in order for the coal to get to the new location. In the process the station got relocated. The company that now owns the powerhouse is also a different company.

U.S. Smelting, Refining and Mining Company were the owners of the generating plant that supplied power to the entire region. They also owned all the gold fields and the gold dredges in the area. In the Fairbanks area alone they had five operational gold mines, which were now all closed.

That afternoon we went to visit the Alaska Pipeline. There was nobody there but they had lots of large posters telling all about how it was built and how it worked. We walked around and took some pictures.

On the way back to town, we stopped to visit Pedro Gold fields and saw the Pedro Monument that was erected in his memory. He was the person that discovered gold in the Fairbanks region in 1902 and on the fiftieth anniversary this monument was erected in his memory. I have a medal that was given to all those present that is dated July 22, 1952. I was at that dedication ceremony.

That evening we saw an advertisement for tours to Gold Stream Mining Camp and that included a tour of Dredge #8 and a lunch at the camp mess hall. We left after breakfast the next morning and headed out to Gold Stream Mining Camp. I had worked as an oiler on that dredge. This place was now considered a museum. I said to Maureen that we could drive there on our own and we didn't need them to show us around.

I had another surprise coming. I didn't know that they had rerouted all the highways. They still had the same names but were nothing like I remembered them. I might as well have been in a different country. Even the road to the University of Alaska was different; it surely didn't appear to me to be in the same place it was.

When we finally got to Gold Stream Camp, the mess hall had been relocated but the gold dredge remained where it was when mining operations ended. They had made some minor changes to the dredge such as entrances to get on board. The mess hall looked the same, except that there were no curtains on the windows or tablecloths on the tables when we lived there. It had also been relocated.

When we arrived, the lady sitting in the ticket booth informed us that the tour had already left and told us what time the next tour would begin. I told her that I had worked on Dredge #8 and she was shocked. She told me that I was the first person that they had ever seen or talked to that had worked here.

She called over the head of the camp and he was so happy to meet someone who worked on the dredge. He asked me if I would go with him and explain a lot of things that he didn't quite understand. Even though he was giving tours; he only knew what he had read from books.

We went on board the dredge and he asked me to explain some of the things that confused him. I told him I would help him out any way I could but on one condition -- that was that he didn't ask me to pan for gold because that was one thing that I never seemed to get the hang of. He said that he could show me that. I told him, "No, you won't, -- so many people have tried but if you want to show Maureen that would be nice." Actually he had someone show Maureen and she did end up with a small amount of gold and they put it into a little locket for her as a souvenir and she still has it and wears it sometimes.

We had a very enjoyable afternoon with them. From there we went to Eldorado Camp where I had worked as a crane operator. When we got there, we saw an advertisement for a train ride through an ice tunnel. Back in the fifties there was no train and there definitely wasn't an ice tunnel. They must have dug a hole under ground somewhere. I couldn't recognize anything and there wasn't anyone there but us. This was the camp that I had the little shrew that used to visit me at lunch time. He was my little buddy that shared lunch with me every day.

I wonder if all that soil that was removed from the bottom of the river, when I was working there, was the base for the tunnel that they later put in to attract tourists. This was the job that I was working on when I was asked to go to the "Edge of Nowhere" as Jimmy Huntington described it in his book.

The next day we went to visit Santa at the North Pole. Santa is present in this huge store 363 days a year; he's not there Christmas Eve or Christmas Day. It is a continuous Christmas theme. I had a long talk with Santa while Maureen was shopping and writing cards to all the children in the family.

He was an ex-truck driver and had to retire because of a severe back injury. He is there full time and he said he absolutely enjoys every minute he is there. You can buy postcards or write letters and have them mailed and post-marked from the

North Pole for a price. I remember when this guy came up with this idea and worked from his home. He sure has come a long way.

After lunch we took a ride out to the University of Alaska and visited the museum. I wanted Maureen to see the state bird, which is the Ptarmigan. He lives in the high mountains in the summertime and came down to lower regions in the winter. He is a very pretty bird. In summer he is a brownish color but in winter he is pure white. If it weren't for the fact that he had two little black eyes and the inside of the ears had a red spot, he would be invisible. He would roost in the trees if the temperatures weren't too cold but when it gets into the sub zero temperatures he burrows into the snow at night. Surprisingly, at the museum, they didn't have a single one. I asked a guide, "How could you not have a bird that represents the state?" The answer that I got was that nobody ever asked about one before so that took care of that.

When we came back to town and were having dinner, I suddenly realized that the Nordale Hotel was missing. That was the most familiar hotel in town and was home to many. Fairbanks was home to many Russians who came there from Russia without family and friends and no home to go to. They kept very much to themselves. They didn't mingle with each other either. They were true loners.

They would go out to camp in the spring and would work approximately six months and when the camp would close down, they would go into town and get a room at the Nordale and live there until the following spring. They would then return to camp. This was their whole life, year in and year out. I wonder what they did when all mining ended around 1968 and the Nordale Hotel burned down.

Breakfast in the morning was getting more and more difficult to get away from. It was more like a party than breakfast. The guests at the Bed and Breakfast were great fun and extremely interesting.

The next morning we boarded the riverboat, "Discovery" and spent several hours sailing on the Chena and the Tanana Rivers. We stopped along the way to visit an Indian village and the tour guide put on a demonstration of all the furs that come from the native animals in Alaska and the clothing they made from these furs.

A young Squaw introduced herself as a native Athapaskan Indian and told us she came from a small Indian village called Huslia in the far north. She was going to show us the different skins and the name of the animals they came from.

I whispered to Maureen, "Did she say she was born in Huslia?" and Maureen said that she thought so. After her demonstration, I went over to her and introduced myself and asked her if she knew Jim or Sydney Huntington. She said, "They are my uncles." I told her I had worked with them and others from Huslia in a mining camp called Hogatza, which was located on the Hogatza River. Surprisingly, she said, "You probably know more people from Huslia than I do." I told her that her uncle owned a riverboat called "The Galloping Goose" and she said that she never knew that.

The squaw that I used to visit in the trading post on the Koyukuk River was her aunt. She was the same lady who had suffered the tragedy of having her baby given away and had no idea as to why. She was the girl that I met at the trading post in Fairbanks Creek that was traveling with the dirty, filthy guy in the pick up truck, which was the last time that I ever saw her. What a small world we live in... We took pictures together and we had to leave as the time was up to get back on the boat.

After lunch on board, we stopped at the home of the previous year's winner of the Iditarod Sled Dog Team. She gave us a demonstration of how the dogs travel. She had about 30 huskies. They had a salmon trap out in the river where they trap salmon to feed their dogs. The river current turns an egg shaped scoop and when it revolves into the water, any salmon within its reach is scooped up in the net. As it continues revolving the salmon fall out into a shoot and the salmon slide down into a big catch box and they can't get out. This is what the dogs live on during the winter months when the rivers are frozen. They preserve the fish by hanging them over wood fires and drying and smoking them.

We returned to Fairbanks in the late afternoon and headed for Ester, Alaska. We had made reservations for dinner at the Malamute Saloon in Ester, -- named after Robert Service's poem, "The Shooting of Dan McGrew". When I worked in Ester Camp, this was our living quarters – now it was a tourist attraction.

I was paying for the tickets and the guy asked me if I had seen the show before and I said, "No, but I have been here many, many times before." I told him that I had worked in this camp. Well, you would think I had said that I had come from Mars. He looked at me and said, "You actually worked in this camp?" I told him that I did, along with hundreds of others.

He said the same thing that they said at Gold Stream Camp that they never met anyone who had actually worked here. This made no sense to me that I was the only one of the hundreds of people that worked here that had come back. He emphasized again, "You are the only one that we have ever met."

We had dinner and the show started. The Master of Ceremonies came out on the stage and announced, "We have an honored guest with us this evening -- Mr. Donoghue actually worked in this camp." Everyone clapped and they brought me up on the stage. That was embarrassing. They actually wanted me to go on their radio talk show and tell my story but I declined that offer. After the show we went into the gold field and it was completely over-grown with brush and trees. No signs of the activities of years ago remained.

There was only one other camp to visit and that was Fairbanks Creek which was about 30 miles north of Fairbanks, so the next day we drove there and couldn't locate the area. We met two guys that were riding an all-terrain vehicle and I asked them if they knew where it was. They didn't but they told us there was a trail over there through the woods that would take us to an area that has some abandoned buildings, but you can't get there by car. My guess was that this was the village that Bobby Hudler and I lived in where the mosquitoes were living between the logs of the cabin we had moved into. The whole area looked like a forest. There was no trace of a camp anywhere.

The single guy who was staying at the Bed and Breakfast was an American living in Indonesia and he owned a business that did beautiful carvings on jewelry, wood and ivory. He also dealt in gold. He showed us a huge rock with gold nuggets embedded in it. At that time he said it was valued at ten thousand dollars. He was interested in Alaska because he said in the remote beaches he could find ivory. He brought down a few boxes of jewelry carved in ivory and wood. The workmanship on the carvings was magnificent and his prices were fantastic. If you saw it in a store, you would pay at least triple the price. We bought several pieces and whenever Maureen wears one of them, people comment about it. We got the idea that he was married to an Indonesian girl. We then had to say our good-byes and we were very sorry that the time was running out.

That was our last day, so after breakfast and shopping for jewelry we took a ride to Chena Hot Springs about sixty miles north. It was a beautiful day for a ride. Chena Hot Springs was a tiny little hamlet with a few houses and a lodge. The pool was used year round. The houses just pump the water into their homes and just circulate it in their radiation. They have no heating bills and no matter how cold it gets outside, the water temperature remains the same.

From Chena Hot Springs there was one more place we wanted to visit so we headed to Nenanna, Alaska. It was a cute little town with quaint stores and we had lunch and visited the Ulu Factory – which makes very unusual knives. They are very sharp and great for chopping anything from fish to vegetables. Each one was curved to fit in a bowl with a nice handle and came with a block to stand it in with the name of the company on it. Of course all the family now has Ulus from Alaska. Maureen uses ours to cut pizza.

We didn't have much time there as we had to return the car before five pm. We would be joining the cruise tour that evening.

On the way back, we got behind a road repair crew going about fifteen miles an hour. We were in a hurry to get the car returned and I put my foot on the gas and passed them by and went on our way, totally ignoring the speed limit.

As we were approaching the outskirts of Fairbanks, a Fairbanks policeman pulled us over. We didn't know why he was calling us over but I pulled over to the curb and asked him if there was a problem. He told me that the state police had radioed him to pull us over and detain us until they got there.

We waited about ten or fifteen minutes until a guy arrived in a pick-up truck – dressed in a pair of shorts and a t-shirt. He came over and asked me for my license and registration. When I took out my license, he saw that I had a New York City mini police shield and a Clarkstown PBA Card from Mike Garvey. When he looked at them, he asked me who was on the job and I told him my brother-in-law and my nephew. He said, "If all your family is on the job - -you should know better." I also told him I had an Alaska driver's license from when it was a territory and showed it to him and he said it was the first one he had ever seen but he still gave me the ticket.

He told me he could write the ticket for speeding which would put points on my license but would give me a break and write it for crossing a solid line. Obviously someone on the road crew called in our license plate, because this state policeman was nowhere nearby or he would have stopped me at that time. In fact, it took him over ten minutes to get to me and he was not in uniform.

He then told me if I wanted to fight it, I could always come back and go to court and plead my case. I said, "No, thank you" – took the ticket and did send in a check for fifty five dollars to pay for it even though everyone told me I was crazy. I didn't resent it. I was as wrong as hell and I figured I owed the state that much for all the good times I had there over the years.

We got back into Fairbanks on time to turn in the car and a representative from the car rental company drove us to the Fairbanks Princess Hotel to join the cruise tour and we had a beautiful room overlooking the Chena River.

The next morning, we boarded the Alaska Railroad for our ride to Denali National Park. It was a long ride and rather bumpy but the beautiful scenery along the way made it worth it. We arrived at the Denali Princess Lodge located in the park. After settling in, we took a bus tour of the park where we got our first view of Mount McKinley. The first animal we sighted was a moose that was very close by. We also saw a great number of wild sheep high in the mountains and many other beautiful animals along the way.

We had dinner in the lodge and the next morning went on another tour. This time we stopped to see Indian dancing and heard stories of their life in this region. Our next stop was at the Iditarod Museum – the home of the famous dog sled team. We had a beautiful view of Mount McKinley in the distance and were very lucky to have nice clear weather to see it. Very often it is obscured in the clouds at twenty one thousand feet high.

We continued along our way and spent the next night at the Mount McKinley Princess Lodge and the following morning the train took us into Anchorage where we spent the afternoon sightseeing and shopping. That evening a bus took us into Seward where we boarded the Coral Princess to start our cruise on the Inside Passage to Vancouver, British Columbia.

Our first port of call was Glacier Bay. We sailed to the bay and watched the glacier calving. That was when the monstrous chunks of ice break away from the ice field and splash into the ocean with a terrific roar. It was really something to see happening.

From Glacier Bay, we took a helicopter ride out onto the glacier. What was scary about that was when you saw the crevices and the cracks that were several feet wide and you couldn't see the bottom but if you should slip and fall into one of them, there was no way you would ever get out and nobody would ever find you. Believe me when you approached one you did it with great caution. The weather was beautiful and warm and we didn't need the winter clothes we brought with us.

After we left Glacier Bay, we sailed to Skagway and took a tour of Skagway and later took a bus tour into the Yukon Territory. We stopped at Bove Island and went onto Carcross and Haines. We had our passports stamped in Carcross and when we got to Haines, I said to Maureen, "You know Maureen I have been here before, I recognize this place." Then I wondered if the Alcan Highway passed through here. That would be the only way that I could possibly have been here.

We stopped into the tourist office and I inquired if the Alcan Highway passed through here and the lady I spoke to said, "Oh is that what they used to call the highway? It's now called the Alaska Highway." So I had been in Haines and recognized it after over forty years. It was a very interesting trip and we went through the trail of the Ninety Eight Gold Rush where so many lives were lost. Many froze to death. We returned to Skagway and boarded the ship to Juneau.

Juneau is the capital city and it is the only capital city in North America that cannot be reached by land. You have to either fly or sail – that is the only option. Maureen enjoyed Juneau – spending quite a bit of time sightseeing and shopping. We then sailed on to Ketchikan where we did more sightseeing and more shopping. When I was in Alaska, the people in the far north always referred to this part of Alaska as the Banana Belt. Our final stop was Vancouver in British Columbia.

All in all we had a fabulous vacation – I visited many of my old haunts, brought back so many memories and it gave Maureen an opportunity to visit all the places she had heard so much about for all those years. They say you should never go back and I must admit there were many disappointments when I saw all the changes that has taken place over the years – Fairbanks is no longer a frontier town.

It did make you wonder where all the years went to. Certainly the trip brought back memories of the wonderful people that I had the privilege of knowing and working with. We worked seven days a week at times when the weather was sixty five degrees below zero. There was no daylight for months at a time. They were among the finest people I have ever known – they were a breed unto themselves.

CHAPTER 25

In Feb. of 2004, Maureen and I drove to Florida and spent a week in Pompano Beach and had a delightful time. We then drove across the state to visit Gerrie and Anthony and Rosaleen and Ray Hoeymans who were down in Florida for the month of Feb.. Nearby to them were Nancy and Ray Goggin and Carol and Bob Schmidt, friends from our senior citizen club so we had a really nice time with all of them.

In March, we flew to Arizona. After spending a week there with all our Arizona cousins in Phoenix and the Campions and Campbells in Tempe, we went on to southern California where we met with Kassie, Jim, Taylor and Michael and went on to Disneyland. We thought that Taylor was an ideal age being four and a half but were afraid Michael was too young at not quite three but we were so wrong. The two of them had an absolutely fabulous time and loved every minute of our trip there. We thought we would never get Michael away from Alice in Wonderland – it was great to see Disney through their eyes.

We then flew back with them to Sacramento. A week later, we returned to New York, in time for winter to be over.

In June of 2004, Liz and Rich Jackson's daughter Molly got married to David Belcher in Puerto Rico. Cousins came from Texas, Arizona, Virginia, Florida and New York for the wedding and we had a wonderful time. We all stayed at the Westin Hotel, visited around Puerto Rico and even had the chance to relax for awhile at the beach. We celebrated Maureen's birthday in Puerto Rico that year.

Kassie, Jim and the children came in for a week at the beach and again spent Thanksgiving in New York. The children have become frequent fliers – quite different from when we were children.

In Jan. of 2005, we again drove down to Florida and this time spent a week on the West Coast on Treasure Island. It was a beautiful resort on the beach and we had wonderful weather. When we told Rosaleen and Ray Hoeymans where we were staying, they realized that their daughter and son in law's condo was just down the road from us and it was not being used that week. Mary Beth and Steve gave them the key and we enjoyed each other's company very much, as we always do.

In Feb., Maureen and I took a trip to South America. We flew from Newark International Airport to Miami, Florida and from there we flew to Rio DeJanerio in Brazil. We arrived in Rio and stayed at the Sheraton Rio overlooking the beautiful beach. We joined our tour group that evening.

The next morning we took a cable car trip up Sugar Loaf Mountain which is one thousand five hundred feet high and later that day took a cog train up Concordia Mountain to visit the Statue of the Redeemer. The statue is one hundred twenty five feet high and seventy five feet from finger tip to finger tip and overlooks the entire city of Rio – it is an amazing sight.

The next day, we took a four hour flight to Iguazu Falls on the Brazilian side. The Falls consist of two hundred seventy five separate falls within a two mile radius. It is the largest volume of falling water on earth. This magnificent sight makes Niagara Falls look like a toy.

We spent the night in a beautiful hotel in the Brazilian National Park and the next morning boarded a bus and crossed over the bridge that connects Brazil, Argentina and Paraguay. In order to view the falls from the Argentinean side, we then boarded a cog train to get up to Garanta de Diablo where the train ride ends. We had to walk three miles through the jungle under a blazing sun with temperatures in the high nineties and humidity of one hundred percent to reach the Falls. We were accompanied through the jungle by a coatimundi. He is an animal that has no fear of man. Emphatically, we were warned not to touch him.

By the time we got to the Devil's Throat where there are fourteen separate waterfalls joining forces and hammering down three hundred fifty feet of cliffs, we certainly appreciated the spray that cooled us down.

That evening we flew to Buenos Aires and arrived at the Sheraton Liberador Hotel. We had dinner at the Argentinean Steakhouse and were then driven to a Tango show.

We spent the next day touring downtown Buenos Aires, which is known as the Paris of South America. We visited the Recoleta Cemetery and the crypt where Eva Peron and Juan Duarte are buried. There were several other interesting stops before we boarded the Royal Princess for our cruise around South America.

After two days of sailing which we thoroughly enjoyed, our first stop was in Montevideo, Uruguay and we did a lovely walking tour of the city. Our rechargeable batteries died and we were unable to find replacement batteries so we learned a lesson to always bring a second set with you when you travel.

From there, our next stop was Puerto Madryn in Argentina where we visited the Punta Tomba Natural Reserve, which is the largest Penguin Rookery in the world.

A few days later, we were to stop in the Falkland Islands, but the storms were raging so badly that there was no hope of going ashore. We were having forty foot waves, so all we could do was wave at the islands.

Our next point of interest was rounding Cape Horn, which is the southern most point in the world. The captain said if we attempt to go around the Horn, we would lose the ship as the waves were eighty feet high. Our only hope was to go through the Straight of Magellan, which we did and it was one wild ride.

We landed in Ushuaia, Argentina, a very nice town located on a narrow strip of land that falls into the Southern Ocean and climbs part way up into the Andes Mountains. I was talking to one of the locals and asked him what the climate was like and he explained it this way, "We probably have the greatest climate in the world – whatever you are looking for you can have it here in one day-- all four seasons. Two hundred mile an hour winds are not uncommon – what more can you ask for?"

We visited Tierra del Fuego, where the Pan American Highway falls into the ocean and this is the southernmost point of the civilized world. I was on the Pan American Highway in Alaska, where it begins and ends 11,987 miles later on this spot in Tierra del Fuego in Ushuaia. It travels through Alaska, Canada, the United States, Central America, Mexico and South America, where it ends here.

The next day, we entered Chilean waters and into the Beagle Canal towards Punta Arenas, in southern Chili. We sailed for two days for a scenic crossing through the Chilean Fjords and the sight of the glaciers were breathtaking.

We arrived in Puerto Mont, Chili and left the ship by tender at four am to get to the airport to fly to Antarctica. As we were approaching the airport, the tour guide received a phone message informing us that there were raging storms in Antarctica and there was no possibility of getting there or landing there. We were very disappointed but I told Maureen that I would be back one day– even if I had to ride a bicycle to get there.

We stopped in Puerto Varas, known as "The City of Roses", and spent a delightful day in this beautiful German Black Forest region.

We spent one final day at sea and the Royal Princess made its final voyage to South America which ended on this trip. We landed in Santiago and visited a Chilean Winery and stayed in the most gorgeous hotel ever – the Hyatt Regency.

After doing some last minute shopping, we flew back to New York and to quote Maureen, "Good bye South America – it was a wonderful trip. Thanks for the memories." We arrived home on March 8th, after three wonderful weeks.

CHAPTER 26

A month later, on April 8^{th,} our grand-daughter, Ella Renee Donoghue was born. All of our family was at St. Luke's Roosevelt Hospital in New York City to await her arrival and Robyn and Mike were thrilled beyond words. It is very nice to have a grandchild nearby.

In Jan. of 2006, Maureen and I drove down to Singer Island, Florida – a beautiful resort on the beach. The weather was gorgeous and we had a great time traveling up and down the East Coast, stopping to see several friends along the way.

Almost a year to the day later, we were again on our way to Antarctica and flew to Buenos Aires, Argentina from Kennedy Airport. After spending a day there, we flew to Ushuaia and stayed at the Hotel Ushuaia at the foothill of the Andes. While there we met a lovely group of people from Australia, who were also going to Antarctica but on a different ship.

We had a wonderful, fun filled evening with them and before we knew it, it was two o'clock in the morning. They were one enjoyable, crazy group and we still keep in touch with them and are looking forward to Ann, Rob and Edna visiting us in the very near future.

We sailed out of Ushuaia on the Polar Star – which is an ice breaker, modified for cruising. One thing that was unusual on this cruise ship was that none of the cabin doors had locks. The captain mentioned this in his welcoming address and said, "We don't have locks on our doors because people that travel to Antarctica are not interested in taking other people's belongings, they are here for an expedition and nothing has ever been taken in our years of travel here."

We went through the South Shetland Islands and spotted our first iceberg – which was magnificent. Two days later, we sailed into the Drake Passage and had our first landing in the Aitcho Islands, off the mainland of Antarctica. It was quite an experience getting dressed in all our Antarctic-proof gear and by the time we got those big rubber boots on, we really needed a nap.

A total of twelve people climbed into each zodiac, a landing craft, to travel ashore. You could feel the cold penetrating right through all the gear we were wearing. We had to wade ashore from the zodiacs but those rubber boots kept us dry. The sight that met us on the beach was truly amazing –the welcoming committee covered all of the beach and available land behind. We were met on the shore by thousands of Gentoo and Chin Strapped Penguins. They are extremely friendly and have no fear of humans. They come right up to you and love to unzip your backpack and try to climb into it. Also, there were giant Petrels, who are very large birds that survive on devouring sick and dying penguins. A fur seal came out of the water to visit but by then it was time to return to the ship.

The next day, Feb. 19th arrived, sunny and beautiful as we sailed into Paradise Bay, in Antarctica. We docked at an abandoned Argentinean Station and were invited to climb a two hundred foot hill, covered in ice and snow. I declined the offer but off Maureen went with some of the other brave ones. They all wondered as they made the climb how they would get down when they reached the summit. Easy -- they just sat down and slid down the two hundred foot hill laughing out loud.

I stood there thinking that on this date fifty-seven years ago, I arrived in the United States and never thought that fifty-seven years later, I would be watching my wife climbing up a hill two hundred feet high of ice and snow in Antarctica and then come flying down on her butt.

That evening we took a sunset sailing on the zodiacs and the crew took us to an area they had never traveled to before. It was a scary, mind-boggling place. We saw unbelievable huge icebergs, penguins, seals, sea lions, and sharks that were all within an arm's reach. We were surrounded by walls of ice that were stories and stories above us, the shrill calls of terns overhead, the burping of crab-eaters on ice flows, the delicate pinks and blues associated with the setting sun and the moon over snow-clad peaks was truly unforgettable. Before we headed back to the ship, ice was forming on the ocean surface, but the memories were warm and wonderful.

Each day was another adventure and we were fortunate to be able to go ashore at different locations. Many people go there and never get to go ashore because the weather is so unpredictable. It can go from nice to horrendous in no time but we were very lucky to be able to make so many landings and see so many different places.

We saw incredible icebergs and some of them were as much as twenty five to thirty stories high and to think that for every foot that is above water – there are eight feet below – a ratio of one to eight. One of the icebergs we saw was definitely large enough to land a small plane on.

Three expeditions each year are chosen to stop at the American Palmer Station. How they are chosen, we don't know but we were one of the lucky ones. It is the largest station in Antarctica and before we arrived there, the Station Manager, Joe, and the Head of Technical Services, Tracey, came aboard the Polar Star and gave us a lecture on the operation of the station and the rules that must be followed by everyone that goes ashore there.

We were then given guided tours of this station – whose sole purpose is scientific study and were warned that nothing whatsoever can be taken ashore or left anywhere on this continent. All refuse that is generated in this facility is stored in sealed containers and about once a year it is shipped back to the states. They are very strict about keeping Antarctica free of all contamination from the outside world.

An interesting point is that there are two identical structures here separated from each other. The reason for this is, in case a fire ever broke out in one building – they must have some place to house the staff or else they couldn't survive in those temperatures and would have nowhere else to go to.

After five days in Antarctica, we gathered on the beach, reluctant to leave this savage and magnificent continent that we were privileged to set foot on.

We then spent the next three days sailing back to Ushuaia, spending time talking with the other ninety five people on board – watching movies and attending lectures.

It truly was an expedition of a lifetime and many times we said we were so happy that we were unable to make that trip the year before; one day would not have done justice to this white continent.

CHAPTER 27

In Jan. 2007, we drove down to Florida and stopped at Virginia Beach to visit Anita and Eamonn, who retired down there. We were able to spend time with Julie, Chris, Alex and Grace, who we hadn't seen in sometime. We then went to Williamsburg to visit Andy and Loretta Hartigan and eventually arrived in Vero Beach for a delightful vacation.

We were able to spend sometime with Rosaleen and Ray Hoeymans and once again met up with our friends from our senior citizen club – Nancy and Ray Goggin and Carol and Bob Schmidt. We also visited our former neighbor, Fred Gritmon, who moved to Florida many years ago and has always kept in touch.

In late Feb., we flew out to Sacramento and spent some time with Kassie, Jim and the children and then flew to LAX to start our flight to Australia. Our flight stopped in Auckland, New Zealand and then on to Melbourne, Australia and eventually onto Sydney. After sixteen hours of flying time, and losing a day when we crossed the International Date Line and then setting our clocks back three hours from Pacific Time, we didn't know what day of the week it was.

We joined the tour at the Four Seasons Hotel in Sydney and the next day had a wonderful tour of the city and a boat ride around Watson's Bay, passing the Opera House and the Sydney Harbor Bridge, also known as the Coat Hanger, by the locals. That afternoon we were on Bondi Beach and of course, Maureen had to go into the ocean.

The next morning, we got up and all the streets were closed by the Secret Service and the FBI as Vice President Dick Cheney was staying across the street from us. Of course there were some small gatherings of people protesting his presence.

The next day, we flew to Ayers Rock (known as Uluru by the natives), in the northern territory on Quantas Airline. What a shock we got when we stepped off the plane onto the tarmac where we were warmly welcomed by a swarm of flies (which we had been warned about) and a temperature of one hundred fifteen degrees.

We had to wear netting over our faces and between the perspiration on your face with the netting sticking to it and the flies everywhere; it was not the best welcome we could have received.

We spent the day touring and by the time we reached the Rock – it was one hundred twenty two degrees. Ayers Rock, which is located about two hundred eighty miles from Alice Springs, is five and one half miles in circumference and rises one thousand one hundred thirty one feet.

The rock looms out of the desert flatness which marvels spectators at the awesome power of nature. The Aboriginal name is "Kata Tjuta", which means many heads, in reference to the thirty odd conglomerate domes that rise out of the rock.

We went to a cocktail hour and drank champagne at sunset and spent the evening at the Sails in the Dessert Resort.

The next day, we went to a demonstration by an Aborigine lady from the Maori tribe, who told us about their life in the outback. She showed us how they start a fire and carry water on their head and picked Maureen to demonstrate carrying a bowl of water on her head. I wouldn't want to be dying of thirst while waiting for Maureen to get to me, but she did a really good job.

After that, we went to the Uluru National Park and took a camel ride; a first for both of us. Lots of laughs but I wouldn't recommend it for comfort.

The following day, we took a bus ride to Alice Springs and saw our first kangaroos, who were nice and comfortable in the shade of a tree and didn't want to be disturbed in that heat. Luckily, we left the flies in Ayers Rock and the temperature was only now in the high nineties.

That afternoon, we took a three hour flight to Cairns and toured that city. The next morning, we took a Catamaran for a one and a half hour ride to the Great Barrier Reef and boarded a glass bottom boat which was fascinating to see what life under water is all about.

We returned to our hotel – had the evening off and went to a "Night Market" which was very interesting. It is like a flea market but is only open in the evening.

The next day, we flew back to Sydney and boarded the Sapphire Princess for our cruise. We were looking forward to some rest and relaxation after the past hectic week.

We sailed out of Sydney Harbor and our first stop was Melbourne – an absolutely beautiful city. I could really live there. We visited the Fitzroy Gardens and the JFK Memorial, a beautiful cathedral and did a wonderful city tour.

We sailed through the area where the Indian Ocean and the Tasman Sea come together and docked in Hobart; originally known as Van Daemon's Land. I never thought that I would see this place, I read about it so many times. This was where the British sent all the convicts from England, Ireland, Scotland and Whales and sentenced them to life sentences if they were lucky (or unlucky) enough to survive the holds of the ships that transported them there. They became slave laborers to British officers who were given large tracts of land by the British government. A large number of the Australian population is descendants of convicts. Today, you would never know it was once a penal colony.

We toured the City of Hobart in the morning and that afternoon visited the Bonorong Wild-Life Park where the kangaroos roam free and love to eat right out of your hand. We finally saw our first Koala and the Tasmanian Devil, as well as some Wallabies and other exotic creatures.

That evening, the Hobart Police Bagpipe Band played while we sailed out of Hobart. They were absolutely the best we ever heard and it was a beautiful send-off as we sailed out of Australia to New Zealand. It was amazing, the number of Australians on the ship that were going to New Zealand for their first time.

We sailed through the Fjord-land National Park and passed through Milford Sound and Mitre Peak. It rises to an impressive five thousand five hundred sixty feet from the water's edge. This area of New Zealand is very mountainous and uninhabited. This rainforest often gets as much as twenty four inches of rain in twenty four hours and the falls form veils of mist against the dark rock and they cascade down the mountains, making magnificent waterfalls. It is shrouded in the clouds and it looks like these mini falls are coming out of the clouds as they stream in every direction coming down the mountainside. It is very, very rugged terrain and in an average year this area gets two hundred days of rain, so the vegetation is unbelievable.

Our first stop in New Zealand was supposed to be Dunedin but we couldn't dock because the winds were over forty five knots and it was too dangerous. Actually, we were back in New Zealand for the second time. Our flight to Australia had stopped in New Zealand about ten days earlier.

We sailed onto Christ Church and after we docked we took a tour of the city. When we crossed over the Bridge of Remembrance, we were entertained by a group of street entertainers in the town square. We sat down to watch them and the next thing I heard was, "Mr. Cool over there in the blue shirt with his arms folded is really having a good time." I looked around to see who that was when I realized they were talking about me. We enjoyed ourselves very much.

Maureen wanted to do some shopping and I sat down on a bench in the square next to a wild and wooly New Zealander. In looking at him, I figured he was going to hit me up for some money but we started to talk and he was one of the most interesting people that I met on my whole trip. It turned out he was Australian living in New Zealand and he had three sons that he saw occasionally – when they needed money he said.. I laughed more in that time and I couldn't believe that we spent over two hours together and I never got his name – nor did he get mine. I do feel badly about that. He was one smart character; talk about looks being deceiving.. There's a perfect example of why you should "Never judge a book by its cover". Maureen took a picture of us when she returned and I laugh every time that I look at it.

We were at sea the next day and our next stop was Tauranga, New Zealand. My niece Maura (Byrnes) Derecourt lives in that town and we had contacted her before leaving home to tell her we would be docking there. She told us she and her daughters would be at the dock to meet us. We hadn't see Maura in about ten years and during that time she married a New Zealander (called a Kiwi) and had settled in Tauranga.

When we came off the dock, we were looking for this jet black haired girl and instead were met by this beautiful silver haired mother of two darling girls. Her husband, Russell, was away on a business trip in Australia and Maura did a fabulous job in showing us around Tauranga. They have an absolutely gorgeous home on top of a high hill and the view from there was incredible. In fact, she was able to see the ship docking from her deck that morning.

The girls were thrilled to be tour guides and took us all around. Ciara was going to be making 1st Communion a few weeks later and wanted to show us the church she would be making it in. It was the most unusual Catholic Church we ever saw; it was built by the Maori Tribe and everything inside was in the Maori language. The statues were unlike anything we had ever seen and the carvings were amazing. The whole church had about seven or eight pews.

New Zealand is magnificent; you would think you were in Ireland, other than the hills and the tropical plants that make it different. It is much prettier than Australia. We spent the day traveling around and ended up at the beach, before we headed back to the ship. Ciara and Niamh both thought they could come aboard the ship with us but security didn't allow that and we left them with tears flowing as we said good-bye. They promised to come visit us in New York in the near future, which we really hope they do.

Our final destination was Auckland and from there we boarded our plane and twenty one hours later we were back in JFK. Of course, I slept most of the way and Maureen read two books and was ready to hit me with one of them for snoring so loudly. The lady who was sitting behind us asked me what I took to sleep that much. I told her I didn't take anything but had a clear conscience and her comment was, "I don't think you have any conscience; I think you died and woke up in New York."

We had a wonderful time – it was a trip of a lifetime and would definitely recommend it for a great vacation. We are so happy that we went there.

CHAPTER 28

On Oct. 1, 2008, we arrived in Rome, Italy. We were there for three days and visited the Vatican, the Sistine Chapel, Saint Peter's Basilica, the Square, the Spanish Steps, the Coliseum and many museums. We then traveled to Civitavecchia and boarded the Grand Princess, for a twelve day cruise.

Our first stop was in Naples, where we boarded a hydrofoil (a craft that rides on a cushion of air), which took us to the Isle of Capri. We then rode a cog train to the town, which is located in an extremely rugged area of steep hills and deep valleys, which made walking extremely difficult. We visited the Aug.us Gardens, which were absolutely beautiful and wandered through quaint, narrow streets lined with cafes and shops.

From there, we visited Sorrento, which is renowned for its manufacturing of wood inlays and veneers. After lunch at a café overlooking the Bay of Naples, we took a bus trip to Pompeii. We traveled along the Amalfi Coast, which is a stunning coastal drive seeing Mount Vesuvius along the way. In Pompeii, we visited the ruins, which had been buried under twenty feet of volcanic ash in the first century, when Mount Vesuvius erupted. It's an ongoing process of uncovering these ruins and they are an amazing sight and a very interesting place to visit.

On our way back, we spent some time in Naples and then the ship sailed for Athens, Greece.

In Athens, we had the honor of being there during a big strike of the "working people" but our driver was able to bypass the areas they were demonstrating in and took us into the city. Athens is very pretty with beautiful flower gardens, trees and wide streets. We visited the temples, the Olympic Stadium and Hadrian's Arch and went to the Acropolis. We also visited the National Gardens and the Tomb of the Unknown Soldier. It was a delightful day.

Our next stop was Kusadasi, Turkey – an extremely busy port. After we disembarked, we traveled by coach to Ephesus, which tradition says that both Mary, the Mother of God and John the Evangelist lived in during their final years. We attended Mass at the Shrine in the Solmissos Mountains that is recognized as the place St. John took Mary after the Crucifixion of Christ because she feared for her life. Mary and St. John are revered by both Christians and Muslims.

Later, we passed through the Magnesia Gate and explored ancient Ephesus on a walking tour. Among the ruins is the great theatre where St. Paul preached to the Ephesians. Even in its abandoned state, Ephesus remains an awe-inspiring city, in an amazing setting.

We then sailed to Istanbul and our bus tour took us across the Bosporus to Asia. This brought us to the sixth continent that we have visited. We spent the afternoon at the Grand Bazaar and you would need a GPS system to find your way around. There are over four thousand vendors displaying their wares and the advice we were given by the staff on the ship is to offer fifty percent of the asking price and settle somewhere between sixty and seventy percent. Maureen loved the bargaining and I pretended that I didn't know her. I thought we would have to buy another suitcase going home from this trip for all the things she purchased.

The next day, we were scheduled to land in Mykonos, Greece but the winds were so strong they were unable to dock there, so we headed to Egypt.

After a day at sea, we landed in Port Said, North Africa. We took a three and a half hour bus trip to Cairo. That afternoon we sailed in the Suez Canal, saw the Nile River, crossed under the Peace Bridge which connects Africa to Jordan and arrived at our first pyramid.

We were traveling in a jeep convoy over the Sahara Desert when our jeep sank into the sand and before long we had sunk to the floor boards. The jeep traveling behind us came to our aid and they got stuck also. Before we knew it, there were four jeeps all in the same predicament.

By now the manpower had grown to twelve but none had a shovel or any tool. They were down on their knees scooping the sand with their bare hands – pushing, pulling, scraping and eventually they got one vehicle at a time moving.

We visited many pyramids, including the Great Pyramid of Giza and when we got to the Great Pyramid of Cheops, Maureen and I went camel riding. I wouldn't recommend any long trip on this mode of transportation but we had lots of laughs. Actually, I wouldn't recommend driving in Egypt because traffic lights are considered a suggestion only and road signs have no meaning to drivers anywhere and lane markers are considered a decoration. We visited many pyramids and the Sphinx and of all the Seven Wonders of the Ancient World, only the Great Pyramid of Giza remains. Now, we had visited the last of the seven continents.

The following day, we visited Alexandria. This city is located on the Mediterranean and we drove along the beaches and visited the Montazah Palace – the summer residence of King Farouk. We stopped at Fort Quait Bay and the Pharos L ighthouse – a beautiful site.

It was a fabulous trip and we returned home on Air France after a stop in Paris.

CHAPTER 29

In Nov. of 2008, Jim, Taylor and Michael flew in for Thanksgiving and that same weekend, Mike and Robyn closed on the sale of their co-op in Riverdale and moved in with us while looking to purchase a home in Rockland County. For the first time in over twenty years, we were all back together again.

In Jan., we drove down to Hollywood, Florida and spent a lovely week in a time-share right on the beach. We then drove over to the West Coast to visit our cousin, Rosaleen Hoeymans and friends, Nancy and Ray Goggin. Ray Hoeymans had died the previous year and we wanted to spend some time with Rosaleen. On the way home, we stopped in Virginia Beach and had a lovely visit with Anita, Eamonn and their family.

Feb. took us to Arizona for two wonderful weeks with family and friends. We are truly blessed to have so many great relatives in the west that welcome us every time we visit there. It truly is our second home.

We got carried away with a hot air balloon ride over Scottsdale and spent three wonderful hours sailing above that beautiful area. We were able to see the sights and sounds of desert life and the pilot often descended to within inches of trees and cacti, much to everyone's delight.

When we landed, we were greeted in the traditional manner, with flutes of champagne and a deliciously prepared breakfast. Since we were first time riders, we were treated to the legendary ceremony that balloonists all over the world have been sharing for more than a century. They presented us with certificates to note this memorable occasion.

The highlight of our vacations in Arizona is when Ned Traver takes us on one of his sight-seeing trips. This is not just a trip – it is an adventure and we never know where we are going to end up. Ned does all the planning and JoAnn, Maureen and I go along for the ride and believe me some of the places we have found ourselves in, don't even exist on a map. Of course, he always says we are going to see a "roadrunner" because in all the times we have been in Arizona, I have never seen one. I question if they truly exist but they continue to send me roadrunners in every shape and form, but no live ones, so I'm still not sure if they are a myth.

In the fall of 2009, we flew to Heathrow Airport in London, England and from there boarded the Diamond Princess, for a 19 day cruise to celebrate our 50th wedding anniversary.

Our itinerary included two stops in Norway in Stavanger and Bergen, one in Scotland in Lerwick, one in Denmark in Torshavn, which is part of the Faroe Islands, two in Iceland in Akureyri and Reykjavik, two in Greenland in Nuuk and Nanortalik and finally docking in St. Johns, New Foundland before sailing home to New York.

When we opened the drapes to look out at Stavanger, Norway, it was like looking at an "old world" postcard with its 17th and 18th century old wooden houses. It was a cold, windy, wet day but we ventured out to tour the city and were absolutely shocked at the prices of everything. For instance, Maureen had bought ten postcards to mail to the grandchildren and grandnieces and nephews and when she got to the post office, where there were 31 people ahead of her, the cost was over $30 for stamps. Everywhere we went, we questioned how do people live in this city?

Our next stop was in Bergen, the Fjord Capital of Norway. Bergen sits in a harbor between the mountains and the sea and is one of the most beautiful cities we have ever visited. There are flowers, shrubs, gorgeous lawns, statues and waterfalls everywhere you look and the city is surrounded by beautiful green hills and every street is cobblestone. We were told it rains at least three hundred days a year so we were fortunate to be there on a beautiful sunny, but very windy day.

After dinner that night, the captain came onto the P.A. to announce that we were heading right into a storm with over 60 mile per hour winds so we could not leave Bergen and because of the weather, he would have to cancel our stop in Lerwick, Scotland in the Shetland Islands. We were disappointed but better safe than sorry.

I looked out the window while Maureen was in the internet café and the water was actually blowing horizontally, the winds were incredibly strong. The crew had to drain both swimming pools as the water was cascading out of the pool, all over the deck. It was a rough night, with lots of rocking and rolling but we were both very fortunate that it never bothered either of us.

After a day at sea, we docked in Torshavn, Denmark which is part of the Faroe Islands – lying isolated and unspoiled. It is a weather beaten island with steep cliffs meeting the sea. The city has a population of about fifteen thousand, living in colorful homes that stretch around the harbor. The older homes have greengrass roofs, which when you add the gardens and parks, it makes for a very picturesque setting. We have never seen roofs like these before.

We had a lovely afternoon touring the city and we thought Norway was expensive until we visited Denmark – this was beyond shocking.

After a few relaxing days at sea, we sailed into Akureyri (which rhymes with Tipperary) in Iceland and once again were met with unbelievable winds. When the captain came onto the P.A. during breakfast, we knew he would be telling us that there was no way he could dock there due to the storm and he said that we would sail ahead to Reykjavik, the capital of Iceland.

The shocking thing about Iceland is that even though it is near the Arctic Circle, it is very green, has beautiful botanical gardens and over two thousand species of flowers make their home there.

Since Iceland declared bankruptcy last year, we were curious how expensive things would be there. Their money is the Icelandic Krona and the exchange rate is one hundred thirty nine Kronas for one dollar. Most items have three zeros after them so when you pick up something for 139,000 Kronas, it really costs one hundred dollars. It sounded like we were really getting a bargain.

They get very little snow in Iceland – they make a point of saying "It is green in Iceland and icy in Greenland." Some of the geologic conditions that make Iceland so unique also make it inhabitable. It is a land of volcanoes and glaciers, lava fields and green pastures, boiling thermal springs and ice cold rivers teeming with salmon. We really enjoyed our visit there.

We spent a few more very rough days at sea and then docked in Nuuk, Greenland. That morning we saw our first iceberg – so I guess it's true that Greenland is full of ice. Greenland is the world's largest island and only about fifteen percent of it is not frozen year round. The center of the island is permanently covered with a blanket of ice that is about two miles thick. If this frozen mass were somehow to melt, the world's oceans would rise almost twenty feet and most costal cities would look like Venice.

The city is broken up into closely knit villages and towns and mutual help is taken for granted. The people are extremely friendly and welcomed us warmly with cups of coffee waiting for everyone in the shops. They are convinced they live in the world's most beautiful place, but we would not agree with them.

It was a day of strolling around, up and down hills, seeing lots of statues – in fact at one point I said to Maureen, "If we stay here much longer they will probably make a statue of us."

Our next scheduled stop was Nanortalik, Greenland and that morning when we looked out we saw many, many icebergs. One in particular was floating quite near the ship and the next thing we knew it turned and headed for the Crown Princess. We were close to docking so the ship was going very slowly and the captain was able to back the ship up and let the iceberg float right in front of the bow. He said it passed within a few feet of us.

We were heading for the bay to dock when the captain announced that a large iceberg was blocking our entrance and he would wait and hope it would move, but it didn't so we couldn't dock there.

Instead, the captain announced that he checked some maps and there was a special opportunity for us that day. He sailed through the Quoronoa Fjords and we traveled to the Kirkrpirsdalen Gold Mine, where miners from Spain were mining for gold. The gold in the crown of the Queen of Spain came from this mine.

This was definitely a blessing in disguise. We had a beautiful day seeing some incredible sights and we were the first cruise ship to ever sail in these waters, so we made history that day. At a certain point, the ship had to turn around as that was as far as the waters had been charted and we couldn't sail in uncharted waters. The sights were absolutely magnificent.

As we headed towards Canada, the weather turned warm and sunny and the fleece jackets came off and bathing suits and shorts started to appear everywhere. We were told that there was an unbelievable storm in St. John's, New Foundland and none of the ships had been able to dock there, so we would head to Nova Scotia instead. I have been to both places and Maureen hadn't been to either so we really didn't care which place we docked. In fact, the only time I had been to New Foundland was on Feb. 19th, 1949, on my way over from Ireland, our plane stopped there to refuel. That was my first time on the North American continent, on my first trip to the United States. At that time, New Foundland was not part of Canada but became part of it about six months later.

We spent a lovely day touring this beautiful city, which is now trying to get back to its Scottish heritage, and the tour guides were all dressed in kilts. It was delightful to sit on the balcony and enjoy a drink on that sunny, warm evening.

I must say, that despite the dangerous seas and the terrible storms and the iceberg that blocked us from docking in Nanortalik, it was quite an adventure. Yes, we missed a few ports but we were so lucky to see places that very few people have been fortunate to visit.

In nineteen days, we covered two continents, sailed over 6,500 miles and crossed over the Arctic Circle. The cruise line called it a trip to the "Top of the World" and for us it was an "Out of this World" experience.

I must add that it was delightful to pass the Statue of Liberty in the harbor the morning we docked, and as always, was great to be back home and especially nice to dock in New York and be back in New City in less than an hour.

CHAPTER 30

Christmas 2009 brought Jim, Taylor and Michael to New York and it was wonderful to have all the family together for the Christmas Holidays.

In Feb., we flew to Arizona for two glorious weeks in Scottsdale. Jim joined us to celebrate his 45th birthday and all the cousins got together at Greasewood Flats for a fun time of celebration. As always, we were treated great by the Campions, the Crowleys, the Campbells and the Travers but I must say the highlight of our trip was our Bisbee adventure with Ned and Jo Ann. I think this time Ned outdid himself as we had the best time at the Kartchner Caverns State Park and boarded the tram for the Rotunda Tour of the caves. We spent a fun filled evening in Bisbee, Arizona and visited the Wall between Mexico and Arizona. We drove all the way back from the Mexican/Arizona border to Peoria and still never spotted that infamous "roadrunner". I am still convinced this roadrunner is a myth although all the relatives try to convince me otherwise.

On April 5^{th,} we flew from JFK to Heathrow and then on to Singapore, for a 32 day cruise aboard the Ocean Princess. Our stops included Kuala Lumpur and Penang, Malaysia – Phuket, Thailand – Chennai (formerly Madras) and Mumbai (formerly Bombay) India – Muscat, Oman – Dubai and Sharjah in the United Arab Emirates – Nosy Bee, Madagascar, Durban, East London and Cape Town in South Africa – just in time to see the completion of the Nelson Mandela Arena for the 2010 World Cup Soccer Games.

We are now official "Pollywogs" – a distinction bestowed on anyone that sails across the equator. We had flown over this point several times but apparently that doesn't count – you must sail across to be given this honor.

As we sailed toward the continent of Africa, we were off the coast of Somalia, which is very dangerous territory because of the pirate activity that has taken place in that region. Because of this, we had to take part in a very rigid drill teaching us how to react if we came under attack. Fortunately, we passed through this area with no problems but the cruise company takes the safety of all onboard very seriously.

When we planned this trip, we figured it would be similar to other cruises we have taken. We truly thought we had seen pretty much all the different things there were to see – but boy were we mistaken. This was an absolute eye-opener.

We came in contact with people from so many different backgrounds and communicated with – or tried to communicate with- so many different accents and dialects. Even though they were always speaking English, we definitely didn't always understand what they were saying but we picked up a word here and there and we smiled and they were as happy as a lark talking to us. Everyone approaches you by asking where you came from and I must say that when we said the United States, we got the biggest smiles. They immediately welcomed us in their own way and were so happy to meet us. When we were walking away, they always extended their hand first to shake ours.

We have never in the past come in contact with so many different customs and religions, and on this trip we visited Muslim, Buddhist and Hindu temples and mosques. We were in awe at their devotion while praying, prostrating themselves on the floor, their dress and above all their sincerity. Some temples we had to be barefoot to enter, while others required coverage of the body from head to toe – not even open toe shoes were allowed. In our visits to the different places of worship, we were greeted and welcomed with a warm smile and in one situation, as we were exiting a Hindu temple a lady placed a dot on our foreheads. What it represented we don't know, but it appeared to be a warm and friendly gesture. Don't worry, we didn't return home with a dot on our foreheads – it washed off. They definitely made us much more understanding and tolerant of other people's customs and religious beliefs.

The thing that surprised me most is that with all the differences that exist in our beliefs, and in how we view things so differently in all aspects of our lives, it is amazing how alike we all really are. I have learned more from this trip than anything I have ever experienced before.

We flew over 20,000 miles and sailed 11,094. This trip truly was an incredible experience.

By the grace of God, I have come a long way from that day when I landed in New York, with less than five dollars to my name.

I've been truly blessed with an incredible wife, two great sons, a wonderful daughter, two terrific daughters-in-law and three delightful grandchildren. Our oldest son, Jim, is a chiropractor, who has his own practice in Sacramento, California. He has two superb children, Taylor and Michael.

Our daughter, Maura, is the Director of Social Work for the Rockland County Health Department and lives in New City. She is a wonderful aunt to her nieces and nephew and is known as Aunt Maura to many, many other children.

Our son, Mike, and his wife Robyn, have an adorable daughter, Ella. Mike is an English teacher in the New York City Public School System and has taught at I.S.143 Manhattan for the past 18 years. They recently purchased a lovely house in Nanuet, a few miles from us, and moved into their new home in July of 2009. Ella kept all of us on our toes while they were living with us last year and is an absolute delight.

To complete our household, we have two West Highland Terriers, Archie and Jack, who constantly remind me of who is boss.

Through the years, the good Lord must truly have been looking out for me because what more could I have wished for..

Acknowledgments:

I wish to thank the following friends for their support:

Linda Barnes, Don Cassidy, Kay Garvey, Bonni and Michael Garvey, Bob Harkin, Wes Roussel, Vinny Sullivan and Ned Traver.

A special thanks to my son, Mike, for encouraging me to write about my life's adventures and above all, to my wife, Maureen, for the endless hours she contributed to this venture, because without her, it would never have materialized.